LIFE IN REGEN(
1811–18

Front Cover illustration: Whitby Bay by Nathaniel Whittock in 1832.

Life in
REGENCY
WHITBY
1811-1820

Prudence Bebb

William Sessions Limited
York, England

ISBN 1 85072 257 9

In memory of Bryan Blackwell
A talented artist and a
kind friend.

Acknowledgements

THE AUTHOR WISHES TO EXPRESS her thanks to the staff of the Whitby
Museum at Pannet Park and, in particular, to Roma Hodgson. She is also
grateful for the photograph of Larpool Hall by Arnold George, L.R.P.S.
and the picture of galleried homes lent to her by Barbara Hawkswell. As
always, the staff at York Reference Library have been most co-operative.

Printed in 11 on 12 point Bembo Typeface
by Sessions of York
The Ebor Press
York YO31 9HS, England

Contents

Illustrations

The Commercial Newsroom.

I

The Wind of Change

A HURRICANE BLEW OFF THE land making it very difficult for fishing boats to reach the shore. As the grey sea heaved, the gale whined down the narrow alleys and screamed across the ruins on the headland. It swirled long coats round booted legs and grabbed at women's shawls. In such weather Whitby people had enough to think about so it is highly unlikely that anybody was wondering what had been happening in London the previous day.

But the news would soon arrive because this was the 7th of February 1811 and the old king had finally lost nearly all his faculties through the disease of porphyria, in those days untreatable.

The day before the gale blew with such vengeance, George III's eldest son was created Prince Regent. Under this title he would perform the duties of king until his father died nine years later. That is how we come to call the years 1811 to 1820 'The Regency'.

In the following chapters we shall look at the people of Whitby during that time and find out how they lived.

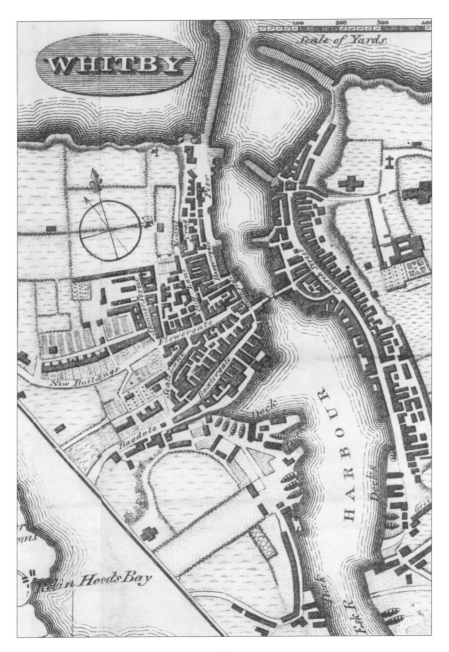

Coach Horns in Whitby

THE MAIL COACH FROM YORK to Whitby travelled by night, crossing the Vale of York, where the silence was broken by an occasional whinny or the call of an owl. When it reached the North York Moors, it rocked on the steep road. Despite the light from whale oil lamps on the outside, the inside passengers could barely see each other in the darkness. From time to time they heard the coachman call to the guard, who sat on the dicky seat with his feet on a padlocked trapdoor which concealed the sacks of letters. Some of them contained bank notes but they were safe for the scarlet-coated guard was armed with a blunderbuss and two pistols. If a mounted figure loomed up on the moorland road to steal those sacks, he would be shot and, if still alive, tried on a capital charge. It was death to rob the mail.

As the coach descended the steep hill towards the inn on Saltersgate the wheelers would strain in their collars and roof passengers would feel

Hull printer's handbill illustration of coach.

relieved when the mail was safely down the precipitous slope. Then the guard blew his 'yard of tin', as he called the horn, and this signalled the toll-keeper to open the gate across the road. Today Barr Farm marks the place where most travellers had to pay before they could go farther along the turnpike road but the mail was exempt from paying. The pike-keeper would hurry in response to the horn because if you delayed His Majesty's mails, you could be fined £5.

When the sky grew lighter in the east, the roof passengers would get a distant view of Whitby Abbey silhouetted on the cliff and see the blue or grey stretch of the German Ocean, as people called the North Sea.

Perhaps it was just as well that the last part of their journey was driven in daylight because the steep descent to Sleights was hazardous at any time. The guard would jump from the back of the coach to the ground and attach the iron brake shoe to the nearside back wheel to prevent the heavy vehicle from rolling too fast down the treacherous hill. At the bottom of this hill, he leapt down again to remove the iron shoe which was then very hot from friction.

His next job was to blow the horn again so that the Sleights toll gate would be opened for the great red and black coach to thunder past.

As it entered Whitby it would only be carrying seven passengers at most; the Post Office permitted three on the roof and four inside but no more. It clattered and rumbled up to the *Angel Inn* promptly at nine in the morning. If it was late, the guard would be fined out of his wages unless the reason was quite unexceptionable. Even when snow covered the moors, the Post Office expected him to try and get the letters to their destination which might mean abandoning the coach and riding off on one of the horses. The passengers were not considered so important as the sacks of mail. Even so, they knew they were more likely to reach Whitby safely on the mail coach than any other vehicle.

They alighted from inside the coach or climbed down the ladder from the roof to enter the *Angel Inn* from whose windows they could see the masts of ships at anchor in the harbour.

The arrival of the York mail gave Whitby people a chance to check their clocks and watches. Its reputation for punctuality meant that it must be nine o'clock and, in case you weren't sure what day it was, the possibilities were limited to Sunday, Tuesday or Thursday; it only came on those days. People who wanted to post letters to Scarborough or Leeds

The Angel Inn.

could use other mail coaches which left the *Angel* three times a week for those places.

The *Angel*, as we see it today, looks very different from the way coach travellers saw it. However, behind the modern frontage the original Georgian building is still visible and used to be four storeys high under a pitched and pantiled roof. The inn fronted Baxtergate with a classical pilaster at each corner and its back overlooked the wooden quay.

It acquired a new landlord, William Yeoman, in 1816. The inn was as useful to Whitby's inhabitants as it was to the mail and stage passengers because it had rooms where public meetings could be held. When speeches and decisions had to be made, it was very pleasant to lubricate the proceedings with liquor from Mr Yeoman's cellars. Auction sales were sometimes held there.

William Yeoman complained effectively about the poor condition of local roads and brought the negligent authorities to book. He was invited to York and presented with a silver-gilt goblet engraved with the words: 'Presented by Gentlemen Travellers to Mr William Yeoman, of the *Angel Inn*, Whitby, for his great exertions in improving (by indictment) the public high roads in his own neighbourhood'.

Mr Yeoman's inn was the most prestigious in Whitby. A few waggons set off from there carrying goods but most of the carrying trade was done from the *White Horse and Griffin*. The *Angel* aimed at high class custom and so had a long room at the back where assemblies were held. Here young ladies in high-waisted muslin or silk dresses danced in sets with gentlemen in tailed coats and white cravats. Sometimes this elegant room with its stage was hired for other uses. The Whitby Religious Tract Society used it in December 1814 for its first annual meeting at which it reported that 28,000 religious tracts had been distributed in the neighbourhood during the previous twelve months.

Besides being a terminus for the mail coach, Mr Yeoman's inn was a posting-house. This meant that one could hire a post-chaise there which was a carriage with one seat facing the horses and room on the roof and at the back for luggage. A chaise could only accommodate three passengers in comfort and it was driven, not by a coachman, but by a postilion. If you wished to go fast, an extra pair of horses could be hired with another postilion, or post-boy as they were called – a misnomer since most of them were old enough to have sons of their own, if not grandsons; but perhaps the uniform jacket with its rows of tiny buttons, effectively concealed a middle-aged paunch.

Print of young lady with harp.

Thomas Sawdon, the landlord of the *Freemasons Tavern*, was the proprietor of a very patriotically named stage-coach. The *England Rejoice* began to run in June 1814 and presumably got its name from the defeat of Napoleon two months previously – a rather premature name since we were fighting him again the next year but a group of Whitby tradesmen celebrated the peace of 1814 at Mr Sawdon's tavern with a hearty dinner and some very drinkable wines.

You could travel south to York or north to Stockton on the *England Rejoice* for £1 or fourteen shillings if you were willing to sit on the roof. Should you want a lift on it for just part of the journey, the cost was fivepence a mile inside or fourpence if you were an 'outsider' on the top. Small parcels could be carried on the coach for tenpence each. The hopeful passenger had to be at the *Freemasons Tavern* ready to be off at six in the morning.

Every Monday and Friday the England Rejoice left Whitby for York, stopping en route at the *White Swan Inn*, Pickering, and the *Globe Inn*, Malton, before arriving at another *White Swan* in Pavement, York, at two in the afternoon ready for dinner.

Those wanting to go to Stockton travelled on Wednesdays leaving at 7a.m., reaching Redcar at one o'clock and finally arriving at Stockton at 5p.m. The coach returned on Thursday morning to Baxtergate, Whitby, where the *Freemasons Tavern* was next door to the *Angel Inn* from which so many coaches departed.

Baxtergate was indeed a district of horsy and leathery smells.

Bridging the River

THE WHITBY OF REGENCY DAYS was much smaller than the present town but covered the area best known to modern tourists. It lay astride the River Esk with the oldest part on the east bank and the steep slope beneath the abbey. Here pantiled roofs, mellow brick walls and wooden steps clustered together providing homes for Whitby's hardworking inhabitants.

On the west bank were more cottages and shops but also some larger, recently built houses. These belonged to shipowners and shipbuilders whose stocks and yards lay on the land side of the bridge where the car park and supermarket stand today.

Joining the two sides was Whitby's bridge but not the one we see now. It was rather like a double drawbridge which was raised by block and tackle. When a tall-masted ship was to sail downstream, local lads would gather to watch as the leaves of the bridge were hoisted. The job was done by two elderly seamen. One of them, Richard Featherstone, was certainly no spring chicken as he had been at sea for 64 years before he was appointed to this job. It was thought remarkable that through all those years at sea 'he was never shipwrecked nor taken'. Being 'taken' meant being captured by the French.

When a ship passed through the open bridge, it was a tight squeeze for the opening was only 32 feet wide. Sometimes the rigging caught in the chains which lifted the bridge and no doubt nautical expletives were carried on the breeze. The jostling crowd needed to be careful; more than once somebody got caught in the ropes and was flung with a splash into the chilly Esk.

Nor were those the only problems. Some fishermen tied their boats to the bridge, doing it no good because, although it rested on stone piers, the structure was wooden.

Whitby engraved by J. Walker 1798. Looking downstream with bridge.

Inevitably, knowledgeable people began to talk of replacing the bridge with one which would open wider so that Whitby's famous shipyards could build wider vessels. James Peacock designed a much better bridge but it would have cost £8000. This bill would have to be paid by the county because the bridge was really part of the road; but when the Justices of the Peace met in Quarter Sessions they rejected the scheme as too expensive. So Whitby retained its narrow wooden bridge throughout the Regency years.

IV

Cobles on the Coast

THE FISHING BOATS WERE MOORED in the harbour on the seaward side of the bridge away from the shipbuilding yards. Whitby's fishermen used cobles – boats specially designed for use on the North Sea. They could be rowed or sailed for they usually had two pairs of oars and a lug sail. Some even had a bowsprit to enable them to carry more canvas and a few had three pairs of oars. The cobles were cleverly made with two keels so the men could pull them up the beach, stern first.

There might have been more fishermen in Whitby if there had been more markets for the fish but the bleak moors separated the town from other places and there was no point in carrying fish far because there was no refrigeration to keep it fresh.

The inhabitants of Whitby could buy their fish at their own doors where it was delivered fresh from the sea. In March 1816 Miss Yeoman bought a cod's head and shoulders from the fish seller and asked her servant to cook it.

Cod's head and shoulders might sound like cat food to us but people in Georgian days thought well of it. They boiled it in plenty of salt and then sometimes placed it in front of the fire and added fat with bread-crumbs. By continually basting it, they were in effect frying it. Another recipe was to poach the cod's head and then serve it with a lobster or shrimp sauce.

We do not know how Miss Yeoman's cod was cooked but, after she had eaten it, the messy dish was removed from the table and taken to the kitchen where the servant made an astonishing discovery. Inside the cod's throat she found a ring with the word GOLD engraved in capital letters on the inner side. They decided the fish must have swallowed it.

When the fishermen met together to share their problems and adventures over a clay pipe in an inn, they would also hear news of their

counterparts up and down the coast such as those from Redcar who encountered such a storm in February 1811 that they were glad of help from the folk at Staithes who fetched them ashore and gave them warm clothes.

In May 1813 the sloop *Constantine*, commanded by Captain Jackson, met an unexpected and frightful squall near Scarborough. The mainmast fell with a terrific crack and it was a fishing boat which went to the *Constantine's* aid and towed her to safety in Whitby harbour.

Whitby's fishermen fished for whatever they could get so the catch varied with the time of year. Salmon and trout, which were netted, were caught from March to August. Crab and lobster were caught in the other months and lobster pots could be seen on the staiths. Many fish, such as cod and ling, were caught on a line baited with mussels.

Some of the hard work associated with fishing was done on land on the scaur where the wives collected mussels. Then they sat in their door-ways opening the shells and baiting the hooks with the shelled mussels.

At night a woman, tending fretful children and hearing the wind strengthen, would feel stabs of fear as she thought of the tossing coble where her man was earning a living for them. It can't have helped her nervousness to recall the terrible accidents of recent times. In a violent storm in April 1815 a third of all the fishermen of Runswick were drowned and the same gale widowed women at Staithes. Whitby people had subscribed to the fund set up to help the dependents for there was no social security.

When a returning coble was overdue, anxious wives might gather looking out to sea and when a small blot in the distance began to take the shape of a fishing boat, hope fought with fear until relief took their place as the coble entered the harbour, familiar hands waved and fish were unloaded on the staith.

Herring shoals were pursued down the coast as they migrated and that catch would be preserved in salt. Some of the larger fishing boats even sailed as far as Dogger Bank but by 1817 there were only nine fishermen living in Whitby.

Many young men, whose grandfathers had been fishermen, went as seamen on merchant ships because it was more profitable. Runswick and Robin Hood's Bay had far more fishermen than Whitby which could provide other more attractive occupations. When the fishermen gathered at Robert Peacock's tavern on the corner of Haggersgate, they probably discussed the advantages of giving up their trade in favour of sailing in a collier or a whaler. Others might speak of the chances of finding work in one of the shipbuilding yards and that is what many of them did.

V

Ships on the Stocks

Up river from the bridge were stores of oak, pitch and tar; cordage, spars and planks. Sawdust blew in the wind and scattered nails lay on the ground. Caulkers packed oakum into a clinker-built hull to make it water-proof. Joiners and carpenters sawed wood and the smith's anvil rang from the blows of his hammer. Here, in the shipyards of Whitby, lads were taught their trades. Downstream, the brig entering the harbour, with bow wave creaming the blue-green water, was coming home for she was built like so many of her kind, in Whitby. Some of them went regularly to the Baltic to fetch the stores needed by the shipbuilders – items such as hemp, which was wanted in Whitby's three roperies. A flight of steps led from Church Street up Boulby Bank, past a row of galleried houses, to one of the roperies. Timber from the Baltic was unloaded near Spital Bridge (not the present bridge, of course) to be used in the shipbuilding yards.

Busy figures, hurrying along Church Street, passed the Seamen's Hospital near the river at Town End and still to be seen there. It existed for the benefit of distressed seamen and their widows. Not far from these elderly mariners was the boat-building yard belonging to William Falkingbridge, for Whitby didn't only build ships; it was the cradle of many boats as well.

The Dock Company owned land on the east bank above the bridge and there the shipbuilders, Holt and Richardson, constructed the *Cyprus*, a ship which the Government used as a transport carrying its red-coated troops to fight the French.

But most of the shipbuilders had yards on the west bank where we have the modern marina and the old railway station. At Bagdale Beck were two shipyards and in 1812 a dry dock was constructed there. Whitby's dry docks were a refuge for ships which couldn't ply their trade in winter

15

when the Gulf of Riga was frozen and sailing to the Baltic was temporarily stopped.

In 1818 another dry dock was made on the east bank at the Whitehall shipyard upstream from Spital Bridge. Anyone walking past the bottom of Green Lane was dwarfed by the overhanging bowsprits of ships awaiting repairs. Nearby at the wonderfully named Abraham's Bosom, hulls were careened and the passer-by might see barnacles being scraped off the bottom of a ship which lay on its side. Vessels needing repair actually queued for a place in the dry dock. Of course, there were some repairs that could be done as a ship lay on the sand but the work might be unfinished when the tide rose and there was a risk of it filling the ship unless it was refloated. So the dry dock, which could shut its gates against the high tide, was in great demand in the winter months.

Insurance companies wanted very large premiums for ships between December 20th and the beginning of March. During the winter days when the wind, catching the white-edged waves, threw feather-like spray into the air and seabirds waded on the edge of the incoming tide, their reflections making a double image on the wet sand, young sailors wandered through the streets and along the quay. They were bound to stay on land whilst their ships were in the hands of other men – those who repaired rigging and mended hulls. Whitby became a noisy place and not merely because of the clanking, chiselling and chopping in the shipyards. Young sailors indulged in horseplay and practical jokes and swaggered along the harbourside watched by admiring lads and younger brothers determined to follow them to sea one day.

Those who walked down the narrow street of Tin Ghaut would face the tall masts of one of the ships anchored in the harbour. It might even have all sails set despite lying at anchor but this wouldn't surprise local people who understood that its sails were literally hanging out to dry.

Other alleyways also gave glimpses of ships. Almost opposite Salt Pan Well Steps was Holt and Richardson's shipyard where there was usually something interesting to see. In 1818 they were fitting the brig *Delight* with a 59 foot high mainmast and a foremast 54 feet high. Knowledgeable boys would note that, if she had to sail in very calm weather, her speed might be increased by adding two t'gallant topmasts, each 15 feet high, to catch the light breezes and she was supplied with yards to take st'unsails so as to pick up a little more speed.

Local lads also knew that there was more shipbuilding to watch on the other bank. Holt and Richardson was the only full shipbuilding yard (as opposed to dry docks and boat builders) on the east bank. A walk over the bridge brought the curious onlooker to the main area for building oceanworthy ships because four shipyards were on the west bank, all above the bridge. They belonged to the families of Barry, Barrick, Langbourne, and of Fishburn and Brodrick.

John Barry's shipyard was close to Bagdale Beck and in 1814 a splendid vessel was built there and named after him. At 520 tons it was large by Regency standards and the only way to get it through the open bridge was by taking off the guards from the rigging. The following year Robert Barry joined the company which could be proud of the success of its ships. The same year that the John Barry was launched one of the Barry's ships, the *Thetis*, was in use for the Government carrying our troops. During the Peninsular War many ships were needed as 'transports' to ferry British regiments to and from Portugal. Whilst Mr Barry's carpenters chiselled and planed in Whitby, did they ever think of the men in cramped conditions on a transport in the Bay of Biscay? Certainly a captain, pacing his quarter-deck, was acutely aware of the advantages of commanding 'a good sailer'. The work done in Whitby's shipyards had repercussions at sea; the careful shaping of a ship's hull made all the difference to the way she sailed.

Two prints of ships from Hull printer's stock of blocks c1810-1830.

But Whitby was not a royal dockyard; most of its ships either traded with the Baltic or chased after whales in the icy waters off Greenland. However, in order to fight Napoleon, it was necessary for the Government to hire ships and another of John Barry's vessels, the *Stately*, was used as a transport in 1814 and was registered in London the following year. Whitby-built ships were often registered at other ports from which they traded. In 1817 one of Mr Barry's ships, the *Hyperion*, commanded by Captain Lashley, made history by being the first Whitby-built ship to sail for the East Indies.

But it was to Thomas Barrick's shipyard that the London returned after carrying troops; Napoleon had been defeated and the London's military adventures were over when it lay once more in its birthplace where Thomas Barrick had built a dry dock in 1812. The London was rebuilt in Barrick's yard, registered in Whitby and ready to go to sea again in 1816. 'The Monster', as people called Napoleon, was now a frustrated exile on St Helena and Whitby's brigs could sail on peaceful trading journeys.

Mr Barrick had indirectly played a part in Napoleon's defeat for he had built several of the transports used in the war, including the *Atlas* and the *Neptune*. He remained part owner of some of his vessels when they went into service but he sold one of these, the *Scipio*, to the Government so in 1818 she was registered in London.

Near to Barrick's was the yard of Fishburn and Broderick.

Thomas Fishburn, whose father had begun building ships in the mid-eighteenth century, was in partnership with Thomas Broderick and their shipyard was on the site of the later goods station. They had already been partners for sixteen years when the Regency began and their association continued throughout Regency days and beyond; it was literally a life-long partnership. Theirs was a lucrative business, as was proved by the amount of the local tax – the Poor Rate – which Thomas Fishburn paid. He was assessed at £40 because he owned Esk House and his share of the shipyard. Between this shipyard and Boghall was a ropery much used by Fishburn and Broderick but they also bought ropes from the ropery in Boulby Bank.

Unfortunately we cannot see the elegant home of the Fishburn family, Esk House, because it was bombed in the Second World War. However, we know that it was near the present railway line and that Broderick later lived there. Alice Fishburn, Thomas's daughter was married from New Buildings, as St Hilda's Terrace was often called; her father was living there

18

in the March of 1816 when Alice's wedding to Thomas Campion took place.

The year the Prince Regent took the oath of office, Fishburn and Broderick's men were working on the *Centurion* and the *William*, both launched that year. The *William* attracted attention with its three masts piercing the skyline. However, in 1815 one mast was removed and its foremast was square-rigged whilst the mainmast was rigged with fore-and-after sails; so the *William* became a brigantine.

In 1812 the yard built the *Pomona* which was a brigantine right from the start and Thomas Broderick remained her owner. It was not unusual for an affluent shipbuilder to be a shipowner as well, making his share of money from trading voyages.

Even if you no longer owned a ship which you had built, news of it would continue to be interesting; it was, in a sense, your child. No doubt Thomas Fishburn felt sad when news came that, in September 1819, the *Canada* had been lost at sea. It wasn't even registered in Whitby for London had become its home port but Thomas Fishburn had built the *Canada* before Broderick went into partnership with him.

Some ships had miraculous escapes but few could compete with the incredible story of the *Esk*, built in Fishburn and Broderick's yard in 1813.

But the *Esk* deserves a chapter to herself.

V I

The Adventures of the Esk

WHEN THE GREY SEA HEAVED into black crests and spilled in white breakers, anxious women would look to the north horizon wondering how
cold and dangerous the Arctic was and what hazards the men faced who
hunted for whales in those frozen latitudes.

That is how Mary Scoresby, a young bride, felt in 1813 when William,
her husband, was commanding the *Esk* on its maiden voyage to the whaling grounds in the Arctic Circle. He came home with fifteen large whales,
the biggest catch anyone from Whitby got that year.

But William was not just a sailor; he was a scientist. Two years later
he was invited to go on a dangerous polar expedition of experiment and
discovery but Mary begged him not to do anything so perilous; she and
baby William needed him.

So he continued whaling. The season of 1815 was not very good but
the demand for whale oil was great. It was used to light homes and shops,
to burn in coach lamps and to cast pools of light over front door steps.

Many of Whitby's whaling seamen saw very little of their homes in
summer for it would be impossible to hunt for Arctic whales in winter.
In 1816 twenty-six year-old Captain William Scoresby commanded the
Esk again and parted from his beloved Mary.

Whilst Mary waited in Whitby, the *Esk* encountered a tremendous
storm but survived it and continued whaling until caught in a pincer grip
between two ice floes.

When those sheets of ice began to part, the *Esk* started to sink; a
jagged spur of ice had pierced her hull and the chilling sea had flooded
into her.

The carpenter brought his pump and measured the depth of water in
the hold – 8½ feet! Every man's face looked horrified; this was their home

from home and their means of returning home and she was sinking. With an energy increased by desperation, they used three pumps, a tub and some buckets and reduced the water level swiftly whilst a signal was hoisted to ask for help from the rest of the whaling fleet.

Then, to thwart their efforts, the hold started taking in more water and soon it was coming in quicker than they could pump it out. At first William Scoresby hoped they could stuff the hole with sailcloth but soon realized that was impossible because a large piece of the keel had been torn away. This was not a mere hole.

In rowing boats, men from the other ships came to the stricken *Esk* and, when her captain explained his predicament, the other captains couldn't agree on what advice to offer. Worse still, their crews already regarded the *Esk* as a wreck and could be heard discussing which sails and pieces of ironwork they intended to purloin before leaving the ship to rot in the Arctic wastes.

But her captain thought differently. He might only be twenty-six but this dark curly-haired young man could be authoritative when necessary and he was no pessimist. He decided that everything must be taken out of the *Esk* and she must be allowed to fill with water so that she sank low enough for them to turn her upside down onto the ice and repair her. No one else thought it could be done but he insisted.

Emptying a whaler meant removing the ship's boats, oars and harpoons; tools, chests and food. For forty-eight hours the *Esk's* men and those sent to help her lifted and strained and carried items made of wood, rope and iron. Scoresby's crew were tough but the toughest were eventually exhausted and he gave orders for tents to be erected on the ice. There was no sense in trying to turn the ship over until she had filled with enough water to lower her considerably.

Inside one of the tents the captain laid some boards on the snow and put a mattress on them. He had been on his feet for an incredible fifty hours and not surprisingly his legs were swollen and painful so that he could hardly walk. He lay down on his makeshift bed in the sub-zero temperatures whilst fog swirled around his tent making everything damp. But he sank into the deep sleep of utter fatigue and for four hours neither cold nor damp could disturb him.

Then he awoke, alert once again and determined to save the ship.

The plan to turn the *Esk* over was too difficult. No matter how hard they worked, the buoyant water still held her. One hundred and fifty men from the various crews were not strong enough to overcome the power of the sea. The only thing they could do was hang heavy anchors from her masts to pull her sideways and fasten her with ropes to the ice. This enabled them to reach the keel, rip off the long broken piece and mend the hole with two sails and oakum sandwiched between them.

All the other crews returned to their ships and their whaling. All, that is, except the crew of one ship, the *John*, commanded by Thomas Jackson. He loyally stood by his friend, brother-in-law and cousin, for William Scoresby was all three to Captain Jackson; his young sister, Arabella, was Jackson's wife.

The two captains made an agreement which would compensate the crew of the *John* if they stopped whaling and towed the *Esk* to safety. Half the cargo, which included the 120 tons of precious oil, was given to the *John* and the other half used as ballast for the *Esk*.

When they tried to sail the damaged ship, she was hardly manoeuvrable because the rudder couldn't work properly. They anchored, laboured to add more length to the rudder and then set sail again.

It would seem impossible to exaggerate the dangers which the crew of the nearly-wrecked *Esk* had experienced. Yet, when the other ships returned to Whitby, the stories told of the *Esk's* misfortune were even worse than the truth. Poor Mary Scoresby heard that some of the men aboard had lost their lives. Whatever had happened to her gallant husband? Shocked and horrified, she became ill with fear.

Fortunately, the following day the *Esk* rounded the pier and sailed into Whitby harbour. Mary literally fell into her husband's arms, gasping with relief and thanking God.

He had already done that. William Scoresby was a devout Christian who held a service on board every Sunday that he was at sea.

Thomas Broderick and Thomas Fishburn, the ship's owners, were disappointed that the catch had been halved but they knew that William Scoresby had saved their ship for future voyages when it might have been left a wreck upon the ice. They gave him £50 as a reward for his fantastic efforts and in Regency days that was a lot of money.

From Whitby to the Greenland Seas

THE UNFORTUNATE WHALES, CAUGHT BY the brave mariners of Whitby, were put to some strange uses. Bits of them were even worn under Regency gowns. Women wanted to look tall and slim but some of them were nothing of the kind and they relied on a corset-maker. It was not easy to turn a pear-shaped lady into someone resembling the statue of a Greek goddess but the Grecian style was fashionable and so 'long stays' were designed to control madam's figure so that she could glide across the room in her high-waisted muslin or cotton gown with all the grace of a figure on a Grecian vase or one of the white figures stuck on Mr Wedgwood's pottery. At least that was the intention.

A stay-maker would create a strong bodice of buckram or jean which extended below the waist to flatten the stomach. This contraption was stiffened with narrow strips of whalebone. Young women and girls were lucky for they only required 'short stays' which lifted up the bosom.

The fashionable lady of mature years, hardly able to breathe in her tightly-laced and boned corset, little knew the agony which another creature had already suffered so that she might wear it.

Expectant mothers could buy a corset which covered the whole torso and, according to the advertisement, was able to 'reduce to the shape desired the natural prominence of the female figure in a state of fruitfulness'. This was achieved with the aid of whalebone stiffening.

To complete the classical look, a modish lady might own a brass lamp modelled on the design of an ancient Greek lamp, which burnt whale oil. Many people preferred to use spermacetti in their lamps, a very good quality oil from sperm whales in Australasia but that was more expensive than the whale oil brought from Greenland's icy waters. Moreover, the Right Whales from the northern seas also had bone plates in their mouths

24

from which the whalebone could be cut for stiffening corsets; sperm whales didn't have these, they had teeth instead.

It was not just the stay-maker who made whalebone corset-stiffeners. A whaler, missing the company of his sweetheart or wife, sometimes used a spare piece of baleen to carve a bodice stay to give her when he returned. More often the men made love-tokens from small bits of whalebone on which they engraved a little picture; it might be a whale but it could be a more romantic emblem. The more prosaic among them might carve some useful articles to sell when they returned to shore. Many of these items still exist as valued antiques. They were called 'scrimshaw' and were created with very primitive tools. A jack-knife cut the original shape but the picture of a mermaid or a patriotic flag, or whatever the young man wanted to depict, was engraved with a simple tool such as a nail stuck in a piece of wood. Some men were able to borrow one of the sailmaker's strong needles to decorate their bone presents.

Most Whitby whalers went to the waters off the coast of Greenland and often entered the Arctic Circle in search of the great ocean mammals which they called 'fish'. In the freezing waters they hauled on icy ropes and rowed small boats in the choppy wake of a whale. By the laws of genetics, their children and grandchildren were surely among the hardiest and bravest in England.

On the grey water, among towering icebergs and white snowfields, the crew watched for the whales that could enrich them. One man would be in the crow's nest atop a mast. The crow's nest was made of wood and barrel-shaped with a seat inside and a partial roof. It had been the invention of William Scoresby's father, himself a whaling captain.

When the look-out shouted from the masthead: 'There she blows!' the crew erupted into frenzied activity for this meant a whale had been sighted. She did blow, too. If the sea was smooth, the look-out would have seen the great creature surface to expel the used air from the two blow-holes in its head and replenish this with fresh air before diving under-water again.

Half-a-dozen men would jump into a boat. It was frequently a Whitby man who was in the front for it had to be someone who was an expert with the harpoon. This skilful task was usually performed by the speck-sioneer, the man whose job it was to look after all the equipment required in butchering whales. A number of Whitby men were specksioneers. The oarsmen were often from the Shetlands and Orkneys where Whitby ships stopped to take on more crew; the Orkney men rowed as well as their Viking forbears.

By the time they were eight yards from the point where the whale next rose for air, the specksioneer was ready to throw his weapon.

The harpoon was like a spear with a barbed shaft and a long rope attached. The other end of the rope was secured to a bollard in the boat. The specksioneer hurled the harpoon with deadly accuracy and it entered the whale behind the head causing intense pain. The suffering creature

dived into the water to evade its pursuers but the harpoon remained entrenched and the rope dragged the boat behind the whale.

This was a terrible time for man and beast. Some whales, writhing in agony, dragged boats for long distances whilst the crewmen were tossed perilously over the cold sea before they speared the animal to death. Its body then floated on the reddened sea as it was dragged back to the parent ship.

Weeks later a pretty Whitby girl might be delighted to receive a charming scrimshaw gift. It probably never occurred to her that the donor had been covered in the blood of a tortured animal before he was able to carve so delicately the love-token which she held with such pleasure.

A very successful crew couldn't wait to tell the folk at home how many whales they had caught so they sent word by another ship travelling home faster. But, with good luck the tally might be higher before they left Greenland.

If a ship returned 'clean', it meant that she had not caught any whales. But, if she had, the jaws of a whale would be tied to the rigging. Then the watching crowd knew that the voyage had been profitable.

As the returning ship glided up the river mouth, small hands waved and a baby would be held aloft in its mother's arms for its first ever sight of the father who had been at sea since shortly before it was born. Days of harsh winds, icy rain and heaving seas were forgotten; friends and family stood at the quayside and this was home.

Besides the jaw bones on the rigging, the ship was decorated with a garland high on a mast. It was made of ribbons and charms which the womenfolk had given to the men before they sailed. On May Day these would have been joined together in a hoop and hoisted onto the t'gallant stay. Faded and stained by saltwater, they still fluttered bravely to show the women of Whitby that their men had not forgotten them during a hazardous trip to the shores of Greenland.

Not all of them returned. In 1812 the ship *Henrietta* sailed into the harbour with sombre news. One of the ship's boats had been overturned by a whale and, although its crew tried to cling to the bottom of the boat, four of them were drowned as it was dragged underwater.

No wonder that the waiting families were as apprehensive as they were excited when the whaling fleet was sighted on the horizon returning to port.

VIII

More about William Scoresby

SOME STRANGE PLANTS BEGAN GROWING in Whitby in 1812; a group of gentlemen started a Botanic Garden in an old orchard. William Scoresby took considerable interest in this project for he had seen unusual plants growing in their native regions. Wherever he went he took meticulous notes of everything he saw and the conditions in the icy northern latitudes excited his scientific mind. Intellectual as well as practical, he was known to have one of the best collections of books of anyone in Whitby.

He was already in correspondence with England's foremost botanist, Sir Joseph Banks, who had been to Australia on Captain Cook's ship. Having studied plants in the southern hemisphere, himself, he was keenly interested in Scoresby's observations.of the Arctic.

On the *Esk's* maiden voyage in 1813 William Scoresby took an instrument which he called 'the marine diver' and he used it to test his theory that the temperature of the sea was warmer below the surface. It was a successful voyage; they caught fifteen whales and the marine diver proved him right – the sea was indeed a higher temperature down below the surface.

In August 1814 Whitby was basking in very hot weather when the whaling fleet was sighted returning home. On board the ship, *Volunteer*, Captain Dawson carried a letter from William Scoresby saying that he had got about 180 tons of oil. By the time he arrived it was 210 tons and they had caught 23 whales. He had also been observing the natural phenomena of the Arctic and making notes about them.

In 1815 William took his Mary to London and, whilst staying there, visited Banks in his Soho Square home. He and Sir Joseph continued to correspond for the rest of Banks's life and the great man was extremely interested in the details of the Arctic sent to him by Scoresby who was also experimenting to improve the accuracy of the magnetic compass.

Early in 1816 William and Mary Scoresby quite literally went up in the world. They moved from their home in Church Street to an elegant house which William leased in New Buildings, now called St Hilda's Terrace. He thought Whitby rents were economical in comparison with many places. He paid £34 a year and was delighted because the house had a pretty flower garden at the front and a useful kitchen garden at the back.

Throughout the later years of the Regency he spent much time recording details of the Arctic and writing a book about it. Each whaling voyage became a source of information for his book. In 1817, with no wind to stir the sails, his ship was becalmed near an island known as Jan Meyer which was also sometimes called Trinity Island. William Scoresby was eager to explore it. His faithful friend, Thomas Jackson, and Captain Bennett of the Venerable went with him.

The beach was covered with lava in various forms so he immediately wanted to find the volcano which had hurled it from the molten magna of its subterranean furnace. Together, they climbed over a thousand feet to the summit of the old volcano. The party could then gaze down into the crater and some of them clambered down to the bottom of it, a descent of five or six hundred feet.

With his enthusiasm for exploring and the curious notes he made, it is not surprising that his book ran into two volumes.

In 1818 Sir Joseph Banks' sister died and, in one of his letters, he told William Scoresby of his great grief. Evidently there was a sympathetic understanding between the famous President of the Royal Society and the young whaling captain. There was also mutual respect for Sir Joseph recognized in the Whitby mariner a very alert scientific mind full of original ideas. William had spent some time in Chemistry lectures at Edinburgh University before he became a captain. He was fired with enthusiasm for a proper scientific survey of the Arctic and persuaded Sir Joseph that one should be sent. The botanist would have liked Scoresby to lead it but he feared that the organizers would insist on someone from the Royal Navy being put in charge. He was right; when the expedition sailed in 1818, Captain Ross and Lieutenant Parry of the Navy were sent to lead it.

Banks also respected William Scoresby's father, who had led a very adventurous life and had done much to make Arctic exploration possible. In many ways William was 'a chip off the old block.' Both Scoresbys were whalers, explorers, men of courage and resource, interested in

St Hilda's Terrace.

Portrait of Sir Joseph Banks.

science, sincerely religious and able to impart their enthusiasms to others. Both were called William.

In 1818 father and son were invited together to dine with members of the Royal Society Club in the capital as guests of the President. This club was composed of various members of the Royal Society and their friends. The ambience would be a luxurious contrast to the deck of an Arctic whaler. Some of the most illustrious brains in the country gathered there to talk of scientific theories and discoveries. But these learned gentlemen knew how to enjoy themselves. Academic discussions took place over a dinner which usually included salmon, venison, beef and claret among other items.

There was another important event that year for William Scoresby: his son, Frederick, was born. In fact, if it had not been for Frederick's arrival, on November 5th, William would have been in Liverpool. He waited long enough to be sure that Mary had fully recovered from the birth before setting out for the western port. He had been offered the captaincy of a ship yet to be built and he went to look at the design, detected flaws in it and was told they would build one to his specifications.

Next year, 1819, everything seemed to be happening at once. He was made a Fellow of the Royal Society of Edinburgh and the publishers accepted his book: An Account of the Arctic Regions. Then William, Mary, the children and their nanny all went to live in Liverpool so William could take command of his new ship.

And there we must leave them because they were no longer in Whitby. William Scoresby had more adventures, wrote more scientific works and eventually became a vicar. The man who had recorded the crystalline beauty of snowflakes and the towering height of huge icebergs had always believed in a divine creator and he chose to enter the church.

IX

Pounds, Shillings and Pence

CONSIDERING THE DANGERS THAT THE whaling ships encountered, it is hardly surprising that they were not eligible for insurance by those insurance companies which had agents in Whitby. There were three of these – the Mutual, the New and the Neptune.

Mr Chilton and Mr Hunter were the agents for the Mutual Insurance Association which underwrote more than 130 ships. It insured them jointly for between a quarter and a third of a million pounds, a colossal sum for Regency times; but not more than £2500 could be allowed on any one ship. The risks were too great.

A sudden squall could do great damage, as it did to the Fame when she was re-entering Whitby harbour. Storms at sea could send a vessel to the bottom of the ocean; so could the enemy. We were fighting France until the summer of 1815 and for two years we were also at war with America. At times other nations were compelled to assist the French and became our temporary enemies. Privateers received Letters of Marque to operate against us and there were pirates. Real pirates.

No wonder that the New and the Neptune insurers, which each underwrote 60 or 70 ships, were not prepared to guarantee any vessel for as much as a thousand pounds. The New, whose Whitby agent was Robert Stephenson, would only insure a ship for up to £800; the Neptune, whose agents were Ayre and Lockwood, wouldn't underwrite a vessel for more than £600. Some of these agents also supported other ships besides Whitby's.

To equip a whaler for a voyage was costly and Whitby benefitted because about £3000 was spent on provisions from rope to meat before the ship sailed. The owners needed some insurance and, since the official companies wouldn't provide it, there were six private insurance offices and many ships were insured by more than one office to spread the risk.

34

The shipowners often had shares in each other's vessels. They could truly speak of what they would do 'when my ship comes home.'

It didn't always do so. A number of whalers were lost.

Since large sums of money might be made and spent in Whitby, some banking facility was essential. But in Regency days there were no cash-points and no multinational banks. The Bank of England did exist but there were no clearing banks. Anyone could set up a bank but not more than six partners were allowed although the Bank of England was permitted to be a company and therefore able to spread the risk and liability among owners of the joint stock. However, it was the only bank which was a company.

The sort of person who set up a bank was someone already in a lucra-tive form of business such as a goldsmith. The banker could accept money on deposit and pay interest; if the customer wished to use some of his deposit to pay a third party, he could write an instruction to the bank rather like a cheque but there were no modern-style cheque books. The banker could lend money and charge interest on it. This was important for people who needed the capital for an enterprise such as equipping a ship for a voyage.

Private banks could even print their own banknotes but it was impor-tant that they had plenty of security for the paper money or else people would refuse to accept their notes. They were usually only circulated in the locality where the banker was known and trusted but not nationwide.

Jonathan Sanders and Sons had a bank at 93 Church Street. It is now a shop but you can still see the old owner's name preserved in the glass over one of its doors. Stand in the Market Place and look at the upper windows which are still much as the Sanders family knew them.

They issued their own paper money with a picture of the Town Hall in Whitby Market on their banknotes and a small drawing of the harbour on the left of the note. As the Sanders were also in business making sail-cloth, people would feel that they had security for their notes but it is likely that they were simply trusted for their integrity because the Sanders family were Quakers, who were noted for their honesty. In 1815, whilst most of Europe was fretting because Napoleon had escaped and threat-ened the Low Countries, poor Jonathan Sanders had other things on his mind. His daughter, Sarah, died that Spring and her body was interred in the Quaker Burial Ground.

Sanders Bank, 93 Church Street.

The following year Spring seemed to have returned to him in December. On the 14th of that month, The *York Herald* reported: 'Singular Occurrence – Notwithstanding the late severe weather, there are at present in Stainsicar Garden, at Whitby, the property of Mr Jonathan Sanders, two rose trees in full bloom; one is the York and Lancaster Rose, the other the red damask rose.' Jonathan Sanders had been named after his father. He and his brother, Joseph, succeeded as owners of the bank when old Mr Sanders died in 1811.

If any of their customers were in London, they would not, of course, find a Sanders bank but their needs could be met because the Sanders had an arrangement with Messrs. Masterman, Peters and Company whereby their clients could have banking facilities. It was usual for a country bank to have 'a correspondent' in the City who would honour their notes and provide for their customers.

A visit to a Regency bank could be a warm and welcoming experience. No machines here, no piped voice telling you to go to cashier number so-and-so. The owner spoke personally to you, a fire crackled in the grate (indeed the banker had probably nodded off beside it), a clerk was writing in a leatherbound account book, dipping his quill pen into the inkstand with soothing regularity.

Some Whitby people banked at 'The Green Gate', a nickname for Simpson, Chapman and Co. whose bank was next door to the house where Captain Cook had been apprenticed years previously. To reach the bank, you went through a little green gate and down a passage. Inside the premises a fire burned in the elegant fireplace of a panelled room.

Mr Chapman was a kindly Quaker whose second son followed him into the business but young Mr Chapman was only eighteen when the Regency began. The Simpsons and Chapmans were gentlemen of

Simpson, Chapman & Co. Bank was next door to the house by the green gate.

property and able to issue their own banknotes which were trusted throughout the neighbourhood. If their clients visited London, they could use banking facilities at Messrs. Barclay, Tritton, Bevan, and Co.

On the first floor of the Green Gate was a very ordinary-looking door but it was really a disguise to hide the safe. In some banks the need to protect valuable securities led to the keeping of at least one pair of pistols. It is unlikely that Whitby's Quaker bankers kept guns for many of the pacifist Quaker community disapproved of the merchant ships going to sea fully armed. Most bankers kept leather buckets handy in case of fire.

Since private banks were usually started by merchants or others who had the capital needed, they were able to lend money to those who required capital for their own business ventures. They would be reluctant to lend where there was little security for, if the businesses of several borrowers failed, the bank itself might go out of business.

Robert Campion was one of Whitby's bankers – a man with several irons in the fire. He owned a spinning mill (now Beevers' Carpet Warehouse) with a steam engine to power the spinning frames. It is a long stone building, with keystone windows, situated in Stakesby Vale. Elegant iron columns supported the ceiling and under this were carding frames

Hope Mill spinning factory.

38

and 'other ingenious machinery', as one of his contemporaries described it. This mill provided 250 dozen pounds of yarn a week and Mr Campion also owned a factory nearby for making the yarn into sailcloth. His sailcloth was stronger than the usual type and he took out a patent in 1813 for his method of making it. Mr Campion called his spinning factory Hope Mill and in 1814 he enlarged it and provided employment there for more than thirty workers.

His sailcloth factory has been demolished but it made the triangular and square canvas which, filled with wind on the 'German Ocean', bore many Whitby vessels to foreign ports and safely home again. Mr Campion's sailcloth factory was not the only one in the town but it produced particularly good material which was correspondingly more expensive than ordinary sailcloth. He had another sailcloth factory at Elbow Yard in Church Street where there were 21 looms.

Nor was this all. Robert Campion was also a member of the Dock Company, a group of four gentlemen who owned land on the east bank containing two docks and a dry dock. They were not shipbuilders themselves but others rented space there and built vessels. In 1816 Holt and Richardson were building ships on Dock Company land. Mr Campion even dealt in wines, too, so it is not surprising that he could afford a grand house.

It was much admired by those who saw it on the corner of Flowergate and Skinner Street, a very spacious stone building with classical details. Some of these are hidden today by a large sun lounge which has been built across the facade of Mr Campion's home and covers what was his garden. The house is now the *Crown Hotel*.

There were two more banks; one, in Church Street, was run by Mr Peirson and the other, in the Market Place, was taken over in 1816 by the partnership of Richardson, Holt and Co.

In the Napoleonic Wars we were literally short of money. The nation could not make enough metal coinage so Whitby, like some other towns, made its own tokens which were used as shillings. They had Whitby's coat-of-arms engraved on them and appeared in 1811. People were quite happy to accept them because they were made of silver and so had an intrinsic value.

There were bankruptcies in many towns and some banks themselves failed but Whitby's five banks continued to trade and enjoy the trust of their clients. Alas! in Queen Victoria's reign Campion's bank did fail but that was years after the Regency.

Campion's House.

Campion's Bank.

X

Spending

WHITBY'S SHIPOWNERS, WHALING CAPTAINS, merchants and neighbouring landowners were prosperous people with plenty of money to deposit in its banks. There is little doubt that their ladies helped them to spend some of it. In addition to twelve 'Perfumers and Hair Dressers', there were a dozen 'Milliners and Dress Makers'.

Many of these shops were in Church Street and Baxtergate, so a lady living in New Buildings could order her carriage to take her to Church Street or even walk with her daughters to Baxtergate if the weather was fine.

It was nearly impossible to buy ready-to-wear gowns in Regency England. The fashion-conscious went to a dressmaker and studied the latest patterns and materials before giving orders for a modish gown and a hat which could be swathed in a matching fabric. If madam had a copy of *Ackerman's Repository of the Arts* (a monthly magazine), she would probably take it with her as she already knew exactly what she wanted copying. Fashion journals usually contained small swatches of the latest muslins and silks to tempt the fortunate females who could afford to order them.

There were some large houses in the vicinity of Whitby where private balls might be held and there were the assemblies in the long room at the *Angel Inn*. The dressmakers would be kept busy sewing seams and applying lace to evening gowns for these occasions. The fashionable silhouette was long and slim with a high waist and, in the evening, small puffed sleeves and a wide low neckline. Married ladies wore silk turbans and feathers. Their daughters had their hair in a small chignon almost on the crown of the head with curls at either side of the face. Ribbons, flowers or pearls might be added.

Lady in evening dress and feathers.

Whitby's watchmakers were also busy making jewellery. Mourning brooches, containing a lock of the loved one's hair were commissioned when a member of the family died. The Victorian love of jet jewellery had not yet arrived but Regency ladies in Whitby had begun to discover the decorative possibilities of their local asset. William Wormald was making jet ornaments in Ruswarp.

Daytime dresses had high necks and long sleeves and were often worn with a paisley shawl. However, when grey waves crashed against the ancient cliffs and white spray flew in the air, salting the lips of those whose work forced them out into the cold wind, a pelisse was needed. This was a long coat, often trimmed with braid or fur. The wives of Whitby's shipowners might add a muff to keep their fingers warm. All this added to the employment of the dressmakers and milliners.

There were straw hat makers who concentrated on the bonnets of the day. Eleven women had established themselves in this trade which probably attracted custom from some of the less affluent as well as the wealthy. The advantage of a straw bonnet was that you could retrim it yourself if you bought new ribbon or a feather the next year. One bonnet often reappeared over many seasons with different coloured ribbons and flowers.

On days when cold rain stung the cheeks and no dog in Whitby needed to wag its tail because the wind did it for them, it was encouraging to spend the time indoors retrimming a bonnet ready for Spring.

The ladies of Whitby were not the only ones to spend money on their clothes. There were seven tailors and nine drapers who also did tailoring so we may be sure that the men were able to order the popular blue tailed coat which was as ubiquitous in Regency England as jeans are today. It is probable that fastidious gentlemen, who had occasion to visit London, came back with a perfectly tailored coat and well-fitting pantaloons from one of the tailors there. However, those who spent much of their time on horseback, could get their leather breeches made at the west side of the bridge by William Swales. The top boots with turned down cuffs

Three ladies with child and toy boat.

43

required for use when riding and walking over rough ground were easy to obtain; there were twenty-five boot and shoe makers in Whitby.

Mr Swales also made gloves. There was a good supply of leather in a town which had many butchers and two tanners. The smell from Frankland's tannery in Church Street mingled with the stench from the boiling of whale blubber in four oil houses, two on each river bank at the south end of the town. In spite of these obnoxious smells, Whitby's inhabitants enjoyed a longer life expectancy than the national average; after all, they had plenty of fresh sea air.

Some of the butchers' shops were on the south side of the Market Place. George Young, writing about Whitby in 1817, noted that there were butchers in various parts of the town and commented: '... a circumstance not very conducive to its beauty or convenience, especially as the cattle are often slaughtered in the shops, or even in the streets. Great numbers of fat cattle, both small and great, are required for our market, and for supplying the Greenland ships and other vessels in the Spring; and there is scarcely any place where meat of better quality can be procured.' It is not surprising that Whitby was able to sell meat to other places. Since the moors separated it from other towns, the meat had to be sent by sea and therefore had to be salted to make it keep. Consequently it was usually ham and bacon that were sent away for sale. In Whitby itself beef, mutton and pork could be bought for five or six pence per lb. It was thought rather expensive when it temporarily cost ninepence and one has to remember that there were 240 pence in £1 then!

Food for the mind was supplied by George Clark, the bookseller. A middle-aged couple, the Clarks were among Whitby's Methodists. George's father, another George, was a local preacher for fifty-eight years and left £250 in his will to the Methodist chapels in Whitby and his library for the use of other preachers. In 1813 Mrs Clark junior died and was described in her obituary as one 'whose amiable domestic qualities have long endeared her to an agreeable (sic) circle of social connection.'

If you felt under the weather, you could visit either Mr Duck or Mr Yeoman, both chemists, who could grind up herbal remedies with a pestle and mortar or sell you patent medicines. There were no legal restrictions on how you could describe what you were selling and the inventors of medicines, sold throughout the kingdom, were never restrained in their descriptions nor modest in their claims.

Mr Duck sold Barclay's Asthmatic Candy. In cold weather, people were persuaded by Barclay's advertisement to buy it because he claimed:

Bow-windowed shop.

'...Its effects are to expel wind, to defend the stomach from the admission of Damps, and to relieve those who suffer from a difficulty of Breathing.'

If aches and pains were the trouble, Daniel Duck could sell you Cumberland Bituminous Fluid, which was for ' the Afflicted with the rheumatism, rheumatic gout, sciatica, lumbago, palsy, etc.' These sufferers were assured it was 'the most extraordinary fossil production, since its happy discovery,' and that it 'has excited the astonishment of many eminent medical characters, who have witnessed its unrivalled efficacy...' Should this miraculous cure fail to help you, Duck also sold 'The Only Genuine Pectoral Balsam of Honey invented by Sir John Hill, M.D.' In bottles at 3/6d or 2/9d, this linctus was said, by its inventor, to be 'unequalled. The Asthmatic and Consumptive may rely on relief.'

45

If a nagging tooth was the problem, Mr Duck could supply 'The Anti-Odontalgia or Specific for the Toothache, which absolutely never fails to give immediate relief in the most excruciating pain.'

Mr Yeoman sold Crystals of Real Cheltenham Salts and according to the advertisement: '...from their Aperient and Tonic Qualities being so nicely proportioned by Nature a continued Use of Them is found to strengthen rather than weaken one's constitution.' It is always pleasing to know that one's remedies will strengthen rather than weaken one's constitution.

There were many cure-alls available including Widow Welch's Pills which could 'create an appetite, correct indigestion,remove giddiness, and are most eminently useful in windy disorders, head-aches, pains in the stomach, shortness of breath and palpitation of the heart.'

Whitby's shops did a particularly good trade on market days when people from the countryside came into the town to stock up with provisions at the stalls beside the Town Hall and bought in the shops what they couldn't get in the market.

Each Saturday was the hustle and bustle of Market Day when women, with shawls over their shoulders and heavy baskets on their arms, came to bring produce for the stalls. Here Whitby inhabitants could purchase their butter, eggs and poultry brought from outlying farms. The farmers' wives could buy their shoes in the same market and anything needed for the big farm kitchen such as jelly moulds, skillets and dripping pans. Fruit

The market hall.

and vegetables from folk's gardens were piled up on the stalls and fish was always on sale.

Prices varied with the season. For instance, herrings might be sold at a penny each but when they were in season you could buy a dozen herrings for a penny.

The market vendors congregated around the pillars which supported the Town Hall. Saturday was a good choice for Market Day as most people received their wages on Friday nights. Some of the produce on sale was worthy of a harvest festival. Alexander Willison, a nurseryman, grew a cabbage which weighed two stone eleven pounds and in December 1813 he astonished everyone again, this time with his carrots. They were the variety named Superb and he brought twelve of them which jointly weighed 3 stone 10 lbs. Most of them had four prongs each and their girth was about 13 inches. People came to stare at them.

As Whitby was surrounded by sea and moor, much of the best market produce came from the valleys between the belts of moorland. The quality of food was less than would be found in a fertile lowland market town but even so Whitby market offered some very good produce. Indeed, there was more than there was space for in the market place so the stalls overflowed into Church Street blocking the way for pedestrians, carts and gigs.

Besides chickens, you could buy turkeys, geese and ducks. Butchers chopped joints, fishwives sold haddock; people bought kettles and clogs and elbowed their way through the throng.

Whitby on Market Day was noisy, crowded and prosperous.

X I

A Flaming Nuisance

NONE OF THE MARKET STALLS sold corn but it could be bought on Market Days in private deals. There were several windmills in and around Whitby. Their tall towers were profiled against the sky, topped by a cap which turned to face the wind. A device called a fantail, which resembled a child's windmill, whirled in the wind and so changed the direction of the mill's cap. Then the giant sails swirled in the gusts and a system of gears transferred that power to a shaft in the tower connected to the great mill-stones which ground the corn.

When an icy wind stung the cheeks and gloveless hands were cold, the sweeps on the tall windmill whirled dangerously fast and the miller had to act quickly or 'she' might be tailwinded which meant that a fierce gust could lift the cap right off the tower. No wonder someone wrote:

> 'From stormy blasts
> And dangers ill
> May God protect
> The Union Mill.'

The Union Mill was the most prominent silhouette on Whitby's west side. It had been set up as a kind of co-operative with 100 members. Each subscribed to its costs and brought their corn for grinding which was done cheaply and so the less affluent people could have good quality corn at a price below the average. John Watson and a committee were responsible for the Union Mill but in 1815 grumbling and criticism pushed Mr Watson out of office and George Young commented:'...the treatment which Mr Watson and others received after long, arduous and disinterested labours, illustrates a well-known truth that he who serves the public, must serve it from a sense of duty, rather than from the hope of gratitude.'

49

The Union Mill was distinctive in having five sails although four were more common. The fifth sweep enabled it to benefit furthur from the wind because it was not possible to make sails extra wide.

Windmills often got named after their millers. The mill at Lower Stakesby was called Anderson's Mill because it was worked by Thomas Anderson. It was a tower three storeys high and used the latest patent sails which were made of openwork shutters to spill the wind through them; there was a system of chains and pulleys to allow the miller to open and close the shutters without having to climb up to the platform and adjust them by hand. Thomas Anderson evidently had a profitable mill because he paid £25 Poor Rate on it. Wren's Mill was often called Bagdale Mill. Its sides were straight, making it a cylindrical tower whereas the Union and Anderson's were more cone-shaped, having tapered sides.Unfortunately none of these three windmills has survived although old prints do give us a picture of them.

Windmills and watermills all made their own noises. A mill was seldom silent. The millstones hummed and whirred; the miller knew by the sounds that all was well with his machinery ... but not at the mill near Sleights Bridge in February 1817. An ominous crackling became a terrifying roar. At midnight orange tongues of flame were visible against the dark sky. Despite the proximity of the river, all attempts to put out the fire failed and the interior of the mill became a charred and blackened ruin. In the morning Whitby's largest fire engine was sent to the smoking scene.

Whitby had four fire-engines, looked after by Mr Lowrie; two were kept in Bagdale and two near the Seamen's Hospital on the other side of the river. A Georgian fire-engine was a wooden contraption containing a water tank and a leather hose; it was pulled by horses and when it reached its destination, onlookers usually helped to man the pump. The amount of water in the tank was scarcely adequate so, unless the engine arrived in the early stages of a fire, it was unlikely to be very effective.

On this occasion the horses pulled the engine out of Whitby uphill and then down to the bridge at Sleights. At least there would be more water available there. The anxious onlookers, feeling the heat from nearby flames, heard the clopping and rumbling of the approaching fire-engine as it came up to the charred building. Although the interior was already burnt out the engine stood there all day whilst the men directed its hose upon the cornmill.

Whitby, from the south.

The mill was a smoking ruin and it was not only the miller who was horrified. There had been stacks of best quality wheat and beans awaiting grinding and they had been destroyed by the fire. The loss of such valuable produce during winter was a terrible event.

Whitby's fire-fighters were more successful in November of that year.

On that occasion the smoke was rising from an elegant stone-built house with a classical portico and a fanlight over the front door; it stood in a large garden and was called Field House. The property belonged to Christopher Richardson who was one of the three Justices of the Peace responsible for maintaining law and order in Whitby. The other two were Richard Moorsom and Henry Yeoman. Each Wednesday and Saturday they sat in their office in Grape Lane dealing with legal matters but Mr Richardson's house was in the west just beyond the edge of Regency Whitby in Upgang Lane and had recently been enlarged which meant rebuilding, the result was so impressive that the York Herald described Field House as a 'valuable mansion'. We cannot see it today because it was demolished in the late 1950s. It was more fortunate in 1817.

After the renovations were completed, the plastered walls were still slightly damp so fires were lit in the grates to dry the rooms. One of the chimneys had a piece of wood in it and this burnt so fiercely that the fire spread into the next room where it licked at a chest-of-drawers and set that on fire burning the expensive clothes inside it. Inevitably the burning chest-of-drawers set light to the floorboards and soon the room became so hot that the windows cracked and broke.

But the fire had been seen quickly and help called. By hard work, the flames were doused and the house was saved. No one had been hurt but poor Christopher Richardson had been having a very hard time. Two years previously, in March 1815, his twenty-three year-old son, Charles, had died. Life does not appear to have been kind to Mr Richardson during the Regency but he remained a prosperous man and a most respected one.

Fires sometimes ruined the lives as well as the property of people. In 1812 John Hopper, a hardworking man who lived in the neighbourhood of Whitby at Overdale, was literally unfortunate. All his property was burnt down for the fire was beyond control. As a result he was left without a means of supporting himself and it was said that, 'He most probably will have to solicit the assistance of the humane and charitable.'

XII

The Whitby Workhouse

MANY A POOR PERSON WORKED from sunrise until it was time to lie down exhausted on a mattress filled with straw. During the day water had to be fetched from the nearest pump. Sticks might be gathered to light a fire; sometimes the incoming tide brought useful pieces of flotsam to the beach. Then a stooping figure, collecting mussels, might drag the wet plank home to dry ready for firewood.

There was no state retirement pension and there was no National Health Service; for the poor, life could be very frightening. if they were unable to provide necessities for themselves, they might receive help from the local fund called Parish Relief. This came from a compulsory rate levied on the owners of property. The actual sum paid varied with the size of the property. Mr Anderson was levied at the rate of £25 on his windmill. Robert Campion was assessed on his spinning factory, bleach yard and land, his house and its garden. The owner of Fishburn House was assessed at £40 but that included his shipyard and a stable in Boghall.

Not that the authorities could always collect the money. In 1812 they received no Poor Rate from Mr Calvart because he was in a French gaol, doubtless a prisoner-of-war, one of the victims of the Napoleonic conflict.

The Overseer of the Poor was responsible for giving grants from the Poor Rate to those who needed them. Sometimes the money was spent on specific items such as medicines from the apothecary. A widow, Elizabeth, who had two children, received boy's clothes and shoes. Another family also received shoes and later the Poor Rate paid for a shroud for one of them; the very poor could not afford funeral expenses. For some years a woman called Mary received money and in 1818 the Overseer, keeping a faithful record in his account book, described her as 'sick'; in 1819 the fund paid for her coffin and funeral. In 1813 Sarah's funeral cost thirty-seven shillings and threepence. A child's funeral was twelve shillings and sixpence.

There were many varied circumstances which could reduce a self-supporting person to one who needed Parish Relief. Jane and her child needed this help after her husband drowned at Monkwearmouth in 1815. A different Jane needed money when her husband could no longer provide for her; he was described as being 'in York Castle', which meant that he was in prison as that was the county gaol.

Hannah Jackson was given payment because she was the wife of a militiaman. The Militia was a branch of the army devoted to protecting this country if the French attempted to invade it. Whilst Hannah's husband was away drilling and learning to fire a musket, he could not work to support his wife. He had no real choice in the matter; quite simply, it fell to his lot. Each place was expected to produce a specific number of men for the Militia and they drew lots for the job. If an affluent man's name was drawn and he wished to pay for someone else to take his place, he could do so. A poor man had no such opportunity and could ill afford to leave his employment. He was given a red coat, a black shako and a pair of boots; his wife was given Parish Relief.

A different Hannah was given clothes for her child but the cost was deducted from her normal weekly payment, instead of giving her the money to spend for fear she wouldn't use it to buy her child's clothes.

Some shipowners and others, who had made plenty of money, moved to the west side of the river where new houses were built. Technically, this part of Whitby was in the parish of Ruswarp which did not have as many poor people as Whitby; consequently Ruswarp inhabitants did not have to pay such a large Poor Rate. So these wealthier people were actually not paying Whitby's Poor Rate. Moreover, the houses they had left were large enough to be divided into tenements and become the homes of several families; tenements were not required to pay rates. All this reduced Whitby's income for Parish Relief at the very time when soldiers and sailors were discharged after the defeat of Napoleon. Unemployment and a drop in the Poor Rate unfortunately came together.

Anyway, for some people the Parish Relief (usually one shilling a week) was not sufficient; they were destitute. For these there was the Poor House or Workhouse, which provided living accommodation, in return for labour. The building was in a field off Green Lane; its surroundings were pleasant but its inmates had lost their independence in return for the most basic necessities of life. There were over a hundred of them although, of course, the numbers varied but they increased during the Regency. By December 1816 there were 173.

In 1818 a new head of the workhouse was required and this advertisement appeared in the *York Herald*:

'WHITBY WORKHOUSE
Wanted immediately

An active, industrious, sober MAN and his WIFE to act as Master and Mistress of the WORKHOUSE at WHITBY, in the North Riding of the county of York.

Persons applying for the situation must produce testimonials of the above qualifications, and it being also of the highest importance to the benefit of the Parish that the labour of the Poor thereof should be applied to some useful and profitable Employment, it is expected that all persons applying will give a particular account in what way they are capable of employing a number of Poor People to advantage, and also to produce testimony of such capability from respectable Persons whom they may have been employed with.

Persons who are, or have been, Governors of Workhouses in other Parishes, and can produce good Characters from the Churchwardens and Overseers of the said Parish will be preferred.

No person with a large Family need apply; and to prevent trouble, the salary is £40 per year with board and lodging.

For furthur Particulars apply to the OVERSEERS of the POOR of WHITBY. All letters to be Post Paid.

WHITBY, October 1, 1818.'

By the time this advertisement appeared the ratepayers of Whitby were already paying 18 shillings in the pound as the numbers of those suffering great poverty had risen. They could hardly expect the new Governor of the Workhouse to get much employment from some of the residents since a number were described as being 'of a great age'.

XIII

Charity and the Angel

WHEN THE DAMP CHILL OF NOVEMBER reached Whitby, it threatened the many poor families whose wage-earners could not get work. Their misfortune evoked the compassion of the merchants, shipowners, bankers and others so these men arranged a meeting at Mr Yeoman's inn where they could discuss the situation.

Their first action, on sitting down together in the *Angel*, was to make donations to raise funds. These collected £1,200, a generous amount by Regency standards, to which another hundred was added later.

It was certainly needed. Some of the poverty-stricken folk were unwilling to ask for Parish Relief lest they were sent into the Workhouse where a number of drunken and disorderly people lived. Others feared public opinion because there were those who objected to digging in their pockets to pay the Poor Tax to support people whom they considered ought not to receive it such as 'lewd girls', as they termed unmarried mothers.

Nevertheless, by 1816 sympathy was growing as people realized that the end of the war had thrown able-bodied men out of work. Many a man returned from the army with nothing to show for his gallant years in the Peninsula except a very faded red coat and the scar of a musket ball; there was no job for him. Those who had been at Waterloo actually qualified for a very small pension but it would not be enough to support a family. In Whitby there would be more veterans from the Navy; they had stirring stories to tell of encounters with French frigates and hand-to-hand fighting on the deck, but they might be temporarily weakened by fever in the Caribbean or permanently limping from an old wound. Their grateful country did very little for them.

The gentlemen of Whitby were more thoughtful. So they sat in the *Angel Inn* that November discussing the situation.

Front and side view of the Angel Inn.

'How do you propose to spend the money?' asked Captain Scoresby (father of William of the *Esk*).

Unfortunately his question was misunderstood and a man indignantly asked, 'Do you think we mean to put it in our own pockets?'

Captain Scoresby, who had never thought any such thing, was the next to be indignant. He considered the comment very rude and later wrote a pamphlet saying that he thought the whole of Whitby could benefit if the money was used to pay unemployed men to work on improvements such as deepening the harbour, building quays for goods to be landed and constructing a new bridge. However, his ideas were not taken up.

The York newspaper suggested that some of the money should be offered as a bounty for fishing catches. This, the *Herald* argued, would help poor Whitby men to earn a living fishing and would provide food for other people when corn and potatoes were expensive.

However, the gentlemen at Whitby decided that immediate help should be given to poor families. They bought potatoes, beef and pork to save them from hunger and coal to warm their damp homes. The Trustees kept a faithful account of the money spent and showed a balance of £4.

Not far below the workhouse were Salt Pan Well Steps beside a yard where there were a number of dwellings. Captain Scoresby senior lived not far away for some time and knew that the inhabitants of the yard were short of water. At his own expense, he erected a pump (which is now in the Whitby Museum) in 1819 and carved on it are the words: 'Suum cuique. Hauri. Bibe. Tace.' One doubts that the grateful woman taking a bucket to the pump was able to translate the latin but, if she had, she would have said: 'To each his own. Draw. Drink. Be silent.' Pumps tended to be meeting places and perhaps the kind captain thought too much time was spent in idle chatter. No more tittle-tattle by the pump!

In 1811 Mr Richmond Porritts died and left money for the benefit of the poor. There were other charities, too, which provided help.

On July 2nd in 1814 the most prosperous tradesmen met together, this time at the *Freemasons Tavern* where the owner was Matthew Creaser and the main object of the gathering was to celebrate the arrival of peace. Napoleon had been defeated by a combination of allies at Leipzig and by the British at Toulouse. Very few people foresaw that he would escape to dominate Europe again. Peace had come and there was no better excuse for sampling the drinks at the *Freemasons Tavern*.

But an altruistic desire to make a permanent memorial to the defeat of the 'Monster' and to benefit the poor as well dominated their thoughts. They had an excellent dinner and some good wines to match it. Then they felt very generous and made a collection '... in aid of the Fund for Establishing a School for the Education of Female Children upon the Lancasterian Plan.'

This school was begun in Cliff Street; there was already a boys' school of the same type meeting in a room in Church Street. The Lancasterian Plan was called after its inventor, Joseph Lancaster, the Quaker son of a Chelsea Pensioner. It was exceedingly cheap in staffing as a teacher taught a small group of children, each of whom then taught another group what they had just learnt. It only cost five shillings to give one child a year's teaching and the youngsters seemed to enjoy it. The children paid 'School Pence' but this only produced 8% of the cost of running the school.

A number of ladies took over responsibility for the girls' school and some of them were confirmed sewers. They spent much time together making shifts and petticoats for 'The Aged Female Poor'. Quite a number of elderly women in Whitby, who could not afford to buy clothes and would not have been able to hobble to the draper's very easily, wore garments made by the slim, jewelled fingers of the wives of shipowners and bankers.

Not that all affluent gentlemen had wives. The silversmith, Mr Webster, was very shy of matrimony. It was Mary Scoresby who changed his mind. She was paying for something in the shop whilst William was away in the Arctic and she accidentally passed over the counter a shilling on which he had engraved his initials. Immediately she asked to substitute another one for it. When Mr Webster discovered how much she loved and missed her whaling captain, he said that it 'almost gives me courage to venture on the serious charge of a wife.'

XIV

The Freemasons Tavern

MANY WHITBY PEOPLE WERE FAMILIAR with the sight of Matthew Creaser in a tall hat and a scarlet coat trimmed with buff facings and gold braid. His knee breeches were the same shade as his collar and cuffs but his tall boots were black.

For Matthew Creaser had been earning a living as guard on the Whitby-York mail coach. He had travelled miles across the North York Moors on the small seat above the boot which contained the mail sacks and bore the cipher of King George III. With loaded pistols, gleaming horn and a leather pouch containing the Post Office watch, he had been responsible for the safe transport of His Majesty's mails through many dark nights. He knew how to fire a blunderbuss and how to mend a damaged coach wheel.

He also made money. Besides his weekly wage of 10/6d, he received generous tips from passengers and became one of Whitby's more affluent inhabitants. He was made a member of the Freemasons Lodge which met at the *Golden Lion Inn*, a larger building then than now. It extended as far as St Ann's Staith and the Freemasons of Whitby were known as the Lion Lodge.

But, though the name stuck, the venue of the masons changed. Matthew Creaser offered to build an inn suitable for them to use. That is how the *Freemasons Tavern* came into existence.

In 1813 the masons moved from the *Golden Lion* to their new meeting place at the *Freemasons Tavern* with grand ceremony. On a mid-June morning Whitby's bells were rung and at 10 o'clock the curious were able to watch the splendid procession of gentlemen walking to church. The Rev James Andrew, who ministered at St Mary's, was also chaplain to the Lion Lodge. For this occasion he preached 'an impressive sermon.'

Coach travel was hazardous in winter.

Then the procession reformed in reverse order with Major Brodrick, who was the Worshipful Master, leading it. With fine dignity they walked to the *Freemasons Arms*. Here, the large room, purpose-built for them, was dedicated 'To masonry, virtue and universal benevolence.' James Andrew made a speech and that was followed by another from Major Brodrick. He commented on how successful the Lion Lodge was and 'in very forcible language explained the principles of Masonry'.

That completed the official business and the next important item was dinner.

With plenty of food and drink inside them, the members spent the afternoon chatting and laughing in what someone described as the 'true spirit of harmony and conviviality.'

Unfortunately the spirit of harmony did not last for ever. It hadn't occurred to the Brethren that Brother Matthew would charge them £22 a year for the use of their new room but that is what Mr Creaser did.

The upshot was that the next year another mason, Thomas Sawdon, became landlord of the *Freemasons Tavern* although Matthew Creaser continued to own the property. Mr Sawdon allowed the Lion Lodge to use the premises without charge.

He hoped to make a profit from providing transport. In May 1814 he began to run a 'Cheap Conveyance to and from York.' It travelled via Pickering and Malton to the *White Swan* in Pavement, York. It left each Monday for the county town where it remained until Wednesdays at six in the morning. Then it returned to Whitby. This vehicle could be hired with its driver at weekends for parties of people who wanted to explore the countryside.

He also ran the *England Rejoice*, which we have already met in the first chapter. One could send parcels on Mr Sawdon's coaches at a cost of tenpence. If the contents were worth more than £5, you had to say so and pay more if you wanted him to guarantee compensation if they got lost.

Already small numbers of people were visiting Whitby for the benefit of saltwater and sea breezes. Mr Sawdon could provide them with an amenity. He advertised: 'The SOCIALETT may be engaged any Day with Horses and Driver, by any party of Ladies or Gentlemen, to go to any place whatsoever, within 21 miles of Whitby.' However, large numbers of sea-bathers had already begun staying in Redcar and Thomas Sawdon realized that a link with that town might be profitable. Moreover, if he ran a coach there it could stop at the *Masonic Arms Inn*, Northallerton, en route. It would seem that the brethren had literally linked up with masons in other places for business ventures. The coach began running in July 1814 and was licensed to carry four inside passengers and six outsiders who paid fourpence a mile; the insiders paid fivepence. The *White Swan* at Redcar was the terminus and July was probably a good month to start because there were many visitors to Redcar in July 1814.

Mr Sawdon provided another service of a completely different character; he was an insurance agent. The London-based company, Globe Insurance, offered policies for Fire, Life and Annuities and Whitby people could take out one of these insurances by contacting Thomas Sawdon at the *Freemasons Tavern*.

XV

Safe from the Storm

WHITBY'S HARBOUR WAS A TRUE haven for many ships, caught in storms as they sailed down the east coast. Indeed, part of it was nicknamed Collier's Hope because the coal-carrying brigs, plying between Newcastle and London, could seek shelter there. It was a dangerous coastline and when a tempestuous sea threw very high waves against the ship, its lower sails could not fill with wind and the ship had to depend on topsails.

If a vessel was approaching from the south-east, a telescope would be trained on the west pier of Whitby harbour. Was there a flag flying from there? if so, the depth of water in the harbour was adequate. If the flag was only halfway up the pole, there was only seven feet of water which wasn't enough for bigger ships. When there was no standard on the flagstaff but a fire burning nearby, navigators knew that it would be too shallow inside the harbour.

Even when the ship's master, peering through his telescope, sighted the flag atop the pole, he didn't snap his telescope shut; there was something else he needed to watch for. A chain of dark rocks reached from the east cliff into the sea. The Sledway, which was a narrow channel between them, only enabled smaller ships to sail that way; a bigger ship must sail wide of those treacherous rocks. The master of a larger vessel continued to train his telescope on the shore; he was waiting until he could see Larpool House, which was on the hill behind Whitby, come into line with the east pier, only then would he order the helmsman to turn to port.

Then one of Whitby's fourteen pilots could come on board to guide the ship safely into harbour. They also guided ships out the haven but, although they were described as 'bold' men, they respected the sea and thought it too dangerous to sail beyond the piers in rough weather. As the pilot climbed aboard an incoming ship, there were surely sighs of relief

Larpool Hall.

from tired mariners standing on a soaking deck beneath a sail stained with saltwater.

It was good to be safe from the rocks but not every vessel managed to avoid them. William Turner, the chimney sweep, had used a rope ladder to haul men to safety up the east cliff. This ladder was kept inside the church so that a rescuer could rush in there to fetch it when the crew of a wreck were observed struggling at the bottom of the cliff.

A panel of trustees was responsible for the harbour but the daily business of running it was the job of William Barker, the harbour master. He had an annual salary of £30 and those who disobeyed his orders might pay a penalty of up to £20. This fine reinforced his authority because he knew the strength of the tides, the width of the bridge and which men owned wharves. It was essential that visiting ships did not moor in the wrong place.

When the wind was fierce ships might be ordered to move beyond the bridge to the upper harbour to avoid the swell. Whilst waves, lace-edged with foam, pounded the shore and spray was flung high, vessels moved into the area between the bridge and Boghall where there was plenty of anchorage. The piers, which did not yet possess any light-house,nor either of the modern extensions, flung protective arms round the mouth of the Esk and had the effect of deepening the water in the harbour. They made a calm haven for ships whilst North Sea breakers battered their stone sides.

In 1812 the harbour engineer, Mr Pickernell, retired and was succeeded by James Peacock. One of Mr Peacock's main tasks would be to keep the piers in good repair. Obviously this could be a very expensive enterprise but there was a fund to pay for it. The fund received about £2500 a year and was composed of the moneys from a government imposition of a halfpenny on each cauldron of coal exported from Newcastle and a duty on salt, grain and foreign goods landed in Whitby and all butter and fish exported from Whitby. So a contemporary could write, '...the harbour has been wonderfully improved, and an effectual barrier interposed to protect the town from the fury of the German Ocean.'

These piers were faced with huge stones weighing tons and it would have required very strong horses to pull them on waggons to the river mouth where they were fastened together with rivets. The mason, John Bolton, who worked on them, later became an architect. Work continued on the piers during the Regency. They were often battered by winter gales and it was decided to add a curved end to the east pier. This would

help the navigators of ships coming from the north which sometimes overshot the harbour mouth and ran into peril on Whitby Rock below the abbey cliff.

Each pier was supplied with a battery of guns. It was not expected that the French would try to land so high up the coast as Whitby but privateers, working for Napoleon, might attack shipping near the river mouth. Perhaps the six eighteen-pounder guns mounted on the west pier might deter them. An extra battery stood on the cliff near Haggerlyth.

In 1816 Whitby made preparations to fire a very different kind of shot. The town acquired an invention by a certain Captain Manby which was intended to save lives. It could shoot a life-line to a sinking ship. A heavy piece of ordnance was brought in a cart. It fired a 24lb shot which carried a line of hide to the wreck where the other end of it could be secured. There was a canvas seat attached in which the crew, one at a time, could be slung and pulled to land by the four men on shore who had charge of the other end of the line. It was necessary to keep renewing the hide because, if it was not fresh, it would snap when the explosion occurred.

Whitby had a lifeboat exactly like Redcar's which had been designed by Henry Greathead. It was kept in a boat-house near the West Pier. Unfortunately it took a long time to launch from the sandy beach but it was cleverly designed. The gunwales were edged with cork and its shape made it unlikely to capsize. Both ends were alike so that it didn't need to be turned when foaming waves broke spuming on the shore.

It is to be hoped that no seafarers were in desperate danger in 1817 because, in that year, George Young wrote, 'At present it is quite unserviceable.'

The water in the harbour was made deeper by the embrace of sandstone piers and when winter winds roared across the clifftops, there were many ships laid up there because whalers could not penetrate the glacial Arctic and colliers ceased trading between September and March. Whitby's harbour became a forest of masts and the shipwrights were very busy with essential repairs.

The aroma of timber mingled with the smell of tar whilst intrepid seamen experienced family life again. When gale force gusts blew down the chimney, it was good to be lying underneath blankets even if the baby was crying and water dripped from the pantiles to splash on the cobbles below. At least, when you walked across the room, the floor didn't move.

During the day a seaman could walk whistling down Church Street to see how they were getting on with repairs to the ship which was his second home.

The upper harbour was south of the bridge. Being farther inland, the water was not so deep and at low tide two sandbanks became visible, muddy and shining; they were called High and Low Bell.

At intervals along the West Pier were capstans and mooring-posts but, when the harbour was full of ships in the winter months, some were moored to dolphins in the central area. In stormy weather trading vessels might take refuge here but would not be unloaded because their cargoes were intended for somewhere else and so the Custom House did not have to bother about their value.

Most ships were unloaded below Church Street but in the lower harbour (which was on the sea side of the bridge) Fish Quay had recently been constructed from Scotch Head to Haggersgate. Beyond it eleven old houses bordered the harbour, a picturesque row of timber properties whose backs overhung the water so there was nowhere to walk between Haggersgate and St Anne's Staith.

Besides the East Pier and the West, which helped to prevent sand clogging the harbour, there were the three inner breakwaters – Tate Hill Pier and Scotch Head facing each other across the river, then Fish Pier on the east side of the water. These were familiar sights to returning mariners

Safe home in port.

and a welcome relief for some of the coal brigs, or 'cats' as local people called them. However, at low tide some ships had to anchor in Whitby Roads waiting for the water to deepen before they could enter the harbour.

The shelter provided there was a mixed blessing because it meant that some ships couldn't get enough wind in their sails to leave it. They added topsails to make the most of the wind but the ship was difficult to control and some smaller ones were actually rowed out of the haven with enormous oars called sweeps.

XVI

Pressed Men

CONDITIONS IN THE ROYAL NAVY made recruitment very difficult. Not surprisingly men did not readily choose to live on a diet largely composed of hard salted meat, dry cheese and biscuits with tiny insects living in them. Naturally few were willing to risk scurvy, flogging or falling from the rigging – all more likely than the ultimate sacrifice of being killed by a musket ball or blown to bits by cannon fire.

Nevertheless, warships required large crews, the biggest needed over a thousand men for how else could one move booms, furl sails, scrub decks or serve guns? The sheer weight and size of canvas, which required manhandling, was enormous but such sails were the powerhouse of a heart-of-oak. Somehow enough men had to be obtained if the French were to be beaten and England saved from invasion. Many ships sailed shorthanded and with some foreigners in their crews but there was a limit to how shorthanded a ship could be.

Faced with a desperate shortage of manpower, the Royal Navy seized men who had experience at sea. Whalers were officially exempt because the country needed whale oil in the days before North Sea rigs and oil tankers. Most ports had a 'Rendezvous' which was the headquarters of the Press Gang, a group of seamen usually led by a lieutenant who went out to 'press men into service'. This meant laying hold of any man they could get and persuading him to offer for His Majesty's service, in which case he got a bounty for joining, or forcibly kidnapping him if he refused.

Escaping the attentions of the Press Gang was not easy but it was possible. When rumour said the Impress was at hand, some young men hid in the woods outside Whitby; devoted mothers and girl friends slipped surreptitiously out of the town with baskets of food. Cottage chimneys, wide enough for sweeps' apprentices to climb, were refuges for lithe young men who might ascend one and come down another into a different cottage.

There were some legitimate ways of evading the Press Gang. A certificate called a 'Protection' was issued by the Admiralty to all men who might be needed for other purposes and could not be spared for the Navy. This included men who had charge of the ferry in any river crossing which was particularly hazardous. At harvest time men working in the fields were exempt from the impress.

Protection certificates gave a description of the man named but if that description was a little out of date, the gangers ignored the certificate. The gangers were not all men from the ships; the officer in charge of the press gang used some local men with a reputation for ruffianly behaviour. This was a fine opportunity for some louts as it was a paid job and also gave the chance of collecting bribes from men who wanted to be left safely at home. It even saved the gangers from being pressed.

On the other hand, ruffians were not all safe themselves. If a tough lad had a reputation for bad behaviour, the local magistrate or other influential person could send him to sea by handing him over to the impress service.

Old Smuggler.

73

When the gangers had seized a man, they took him to the Rendezvous where the officer in charge would issue a certificate saying he was fit to serve in the Navy. He had to be exceptionally unfit not to be so certified, although a hernia (which they called a rupture) would effectively disqualify him because he couldn't climb the ratlines and would be nearly useless in a gun crew. It was not unknown for a man to mutilate himself rather than serve on board His Majesty's Ships.

There is a little doubt about the actual position of Whitby's Rendezvous. Some think it was the *Shiplaunch Inn*, a charming low-ceilinged building in Baxtergate next to Loggerhead's Yard and now a pleasant eating place. Smugglers almost certainly used that haunt which has an underground tunnel. Other opinions give the position of the 'Rendezvous', as Whitby people called it, on the old Boots Corner which is south-west of the end of the bridge and was then called the *Bridge Inn*. For some time the *Bridge Inn* was nicknamed 'Randyvous House'.

The captured men were probably housed temporarily in the basement of the present *Dolphin Hotel*, formerly known as Clarksons. It would certainly be unsafe to retain them at the Rendezvous from which their friends could rescue them since it was a public inn.

On nights when lanterns flickered and deep shadows fell across narrow ghauts whilst a luminous moon rode high above the sea, prudent young men stayed indoors, especially if they were fishermen and therefore particularly attractive to the Navy. No wonder that there were far less fishermen in Whitby than the neighbouring coastal villages.

XVII

The Hazards of War

VETERANS FROM THE BATTLE OF Trafalgar walked along Whitby's narrow streets in Regency days. Men, who had been temporarily deafened by the thunder of a broadside in a confined space and who had been unable to see their wounded comrades through the battle-smoke, returned to a town which was familiar with the guns which armed a merchantman in wartime; but even they could not envisage the effects of fifty-six ships-of-the-line engaged in lethal conflict. They would probably cheer at the tale of a French ship blown up in the water but they hadn't tried to rescue badly wounded men from the scattered wreckage. No one who had not been there could really understand, although, with the passing of years, it became more bearable to talk of it and George, who had served at Trafalgar in 1805 and later sold bread in Whitby, knew how to horrify his listeners. 'The blood, sir, came up to our ankles,' he would tell them with relish.

One of Nelson's Band of Brothers, as he called his captains, was Robert Moorsom whose father, Richard Moorsom, owned Airy Hill, a fine house on the outer edge of Whitby designed by Kerr, the York architect. Robert Moorsom had particular expertise and knowledge of gunnery and he'd been given command of a new ship, the *Revenge*, with seventy-four cannon aboard. As the *Revenge* bore down on the French line-of-battle, she received shots from the enemy and the crew would have liked to return fire immediately but Robert Moorsom knew better. He forbade his men to shoot until he signalled with a burst of fire from the carronades on his quarter-deck. 'We shall want all our shot when we get close in,' he said.

The *Revenge* fought against three ships at once, two French and one Spanish. It was surprising that a slight facial wound was the only injury which her daring captain suffered. He was a member of the masonic Lion Lodge in Whitby and, when news of the battle reached them, they drank his health with pride.

Ready to repel Boney.

During the Regency he became an admiral and Master-General of the Ordnance so he, his wife and their small children, had to live in the south although they continued to own some land near Ruswarp. In January 1815 Robert was knighted and there was great pride in Whitby because its heroic son was now Admiral Sir Robert Moorsom, K.C.B.

A bar shot, which had sliced into the *Revenge* at Trafalgar, was brought home and made into a sundial for Richard Moorsom's garden. It is now in the Pannett Park Museum.

From 1812 to 1814 the hazards affecting seamen increased because we were at war with America as well as France. The dangers were experienced by merchant ships, too. In 1813 William Gates, master of the brig, *Daphne*, was on his way from Whitby to Archangel when his voyage was cut short by an American frigate, the *President*, and he was captured.

Commander Rodgers, captain of the *President*, released him on parole and gave him a certificate to prove it. William Gates had given his word of honour that he would not serve against America unless an American prisoner-of-war could be exchanged for him. At least he wasn't incarcerated in France or Russia as some of Whitby's mariners were.

But he did not get straight home for he had no ship. Commander Rodgers, after his crew had plundered it, sank the *Daphne*.

Next day fortune favoured Captain Gates. A whaler appeared on the horizon, returning from Greenland with eight whales aboard. It was the *Eliza Swan* under the command of Captain Young from Montrose. Commander Rodgers ordered his crew to attack and they boarded the whaler. Soon Captain Young was also a prisoner on the *President* but he was able to buy his freedom; he had enough money with him to pay his own ransom of £5000. Rodgers instructed him to take Captain Gates to Montrose but, before the *Eliza Swan* set sail again, the Americans replenished their stores by helping themselves to beef, ham and a ton of bread plus spare sails, rope, a small boat and other useful items.

One can readily imagine the catalogue of grievances which Gates and Young shared about the American ship as they sat together in Captain Young's cabin. Next day they were hailed by another whaler, the *Fountain*, commanded by Captain Barton, who was making for Whitby with five whales aboard. They gave him all their news and he returned to Whitby where he was able to explain that eventually William Gates would be back home.

Seamen could even get into trouble on land. In December 1816 a couple of young sailors, ashore for awhile in Whitby, decided to visit an elderly aunt who lived in Malton. They had no transport but set off with enthusiasm trudging along Saltersgate, over the earth-brown moors and down through valleys bronzed by last season's bracken. By the time they reached Pickering, they were very tired but they had come too far to turn back without seeing the old lady. Besides, they hadn't enough money for food or a night's lodging so they broke into a stable where a grey horse was installed. They found a saddle and bridle, led their borrowed mount outside and set off again for Malton.

The horse belonged to a bailiff who soon discovered that it was missing. He called out the special constables and soon a hue and cry was raised. Meanwhile the sailor lads had reached Malton, left the grey horse overnight at an inn and genuinely meant to return it next day. Unfortunately for their scheme, the angry bailiff eventually found them. However, their sincere intention of returning the horse was believed and they were discharged after being told in very definite language never again to borrow anything without permission.

XVIII

Money from the Rocks

SLOOPS, BUILT IN WHITBY'S SHIPYARDS, transported alum along the coast. They also took Newcastle coal and other necessities for working the alum to the 'alum mines' which were mostly near the shore at places such as Ravenscar. Some of these alum works were near Whitby; the nearest was at Sandsend.

Alum is a mixture of aluminium, potassium and sodium. It improves the properties of natural fabrics, enabling them to absorb dyes. As a result the colours last well and are bright. Some deep shades were wanted for gentlemen's coats, chintz bedhangings and ladies' morning dresses. Obviously alum was very valuable to the cloth industry and the coast from Scarborough north to the Tees was an excellent source of alum which was found in the rock.

Working in the alum industry could be an incredibly energetic job. Extracting the blue shale meant using a pick to break up the rock. That shale (known as Upper Blue Lias) had to be moved away from the mine so men filled barrows and wheeled them at speed along planks to the fires where the shale was burnt. The labourers were paid according to how much weight they managed to move – a quarter, a half or a full barrow. It is hard to imagine how anyone could hurry with a barrowful of rock but they even ran whilst an overseer nearby calculated how much they were moving.

The bonfires burnt for weeks reducing the shale to cinders and ash. Then it was moved into pits where water was poured over it to make the alum dissolve out of the ash. Men stirred this with long poles. It was washed several times until it reached the correct weight which indicated that it had been sufficiently purified. Next it was taken to a boiler house.

The Alum Works.

After bubbling for long enough, it was cooled and clear crystals were produced. These were pure enough for use as a mordant in the textile industry.

Fortunately for Whitby's shipbuilders, it was more efficient to take away the finished product by sea than to move it over the rough roads of Georgian England.

XIX

Babies, Brides and Burials

WHEN A WHITBY MOTHER TOOK her new baby into a neighbour's house, the infant would be presented with an egg, a roll and some salt.

The baby was baptised in church; fun and celebrations followed the service. These included eating cheese with gingerbread and cordials. The first piece of gingerbread would be cut into small pieces, enough for each unmarried girl present to have one. According to local tradition this would induce the young lady to dream of the man she would eventually marry.

Very poor families would have difficulty in providing for the needs of a pregnant mother or a new baby. A committee of Whitby ladies, called The Female Charity, raised funds to help 'Married women at the time of their lying-in'. The secretary and treasurer were responsible for disbursing the funds.

Weddings might take place within sight and sound of the sea at St Mary's Church on the east cliff.

In October 1812 twenty-three year-old Mary Robson was married to William Sherwood who was a fifty-two year-old farmer at Stakesby; his brother was a miller in Scarborough.

Wedding customs were rather different from nowadays. Bridal veils were only just coming into fashion and most brides wore bonnets. On the 30th October 1813 Catherine Bolton, the second daughter of one of Whitby's shipowners, married Captain Frankland, an officer in the 5th North York Local Militia, who may have worn his scarlet tunic for the occasion.

Wedding cake was usually called 'bride cake' and pieces were sent to friends. It was believed that it had the same powers as the gingerbread at christenings but its use at weddings seems to have been decidedly unhygienic and crumbly. Small pieces (and they were surely *very* small) were passed through the wedding ring nine times before being given to each

St Mary's Church.

of the young ladies for use as 'Dreaming Bread', so that the girl would dream of her own future husband.

More sophisticated families celebrated by the bride receiving morning calls from her friends for two or three days after the wedding; and for three evenings after their marriage she and her husband sat receiving company. Afterwards she returned the calls accompanied by her bridesmaid.

In 1818 William Yeoman, son of the landlord of the *Angel Inn*, married the daughter of William Robinson, the butcher. Theirs was a summer wedding.

The summer of 1814 saw the wedding of Miss Featherstone, who was the daughter of one of Whitby's shipowners. She married a Sunderland corn-factor, Isaac Ayton.

Also in 1814, in a busy week when there were three weddings, Robert Medd, of the firm which printed and sold books in Whitby, married a Whitby girl, Miss Fleck. He would have been familiar with Richard Winter, who wrote some scientific papers besides being the author of *The Harp of St Hilda*. Richard Winter died in July, the same month as the bookseller's wedding.

When someone died in Whitby, certain customs were faithfully followed. Black gloves would be sent to close friends who would gather at the house before the funeral. Some of the women, wearing white, would hand round wine and sugary biscuits. Then the procession started with the women in front wearing knots of white ribbon; next the neighbours lifted the coffin and trod carefully. They had to carry their burden up the long flight of steps from Henrietta Street to the church above the sea. It would, of course, have been easier to go along Green Lane but most people insisted that their mortal remains should be borne up the steep hill which they had so often climbed over the years. The bearers had to rest at intervals and, as one climbs the steps today, one can see the stopping places where the faithful supporters paused to regain their breath and relax tensed muscles.

It would be a relief to reach the door of St Mary's Church and enter it to hear the reassuring words: 'I am the Resurrection and the Life.' After the service, the bearers carried their neighbour's coffin to its grave in the churchyard where incoming tides might be heard and gulls wheeled overhead.

More affluent people used a hearse, pulled by horses wearing black plumes, which conveyed the coffin up Green Lane for a morning service.

The coffin was lifted from the hearse by 'porters' who carried it into church whilst male relations and friends held a pall over it. These gentlemen wore black gloves and black silk scarves, unless the person had died unmarried in which case they wore white ones. The ladies of these 'genteel' families did not attend funerals.

Sadly, less than five years after his wedding, Robert Medd's funeral took place in January 1819. The York newspapers recorded: 'On Tuesday morning, at Whitby, in the 28th year of his age, Mr Robert Medd, bookseller, printer, and etc. He was a man deservedly and generally respected, and has died lamented by those who knew him. He has left an amiable and disconsolate widow in a state of pregnancy, with two children to lament his loss.'

There were several sudden deaths. In 1819 the solicitor, John Marshall, died at Ruswarp when his horse threw him.

In the Spring of 1815 Mrs Elizabeth Chandler died and her obituary stated, 'Her death was awfully sudden, while sitting at tea she sunk down from her chair and instantly expired.'

In October 1817 Cornelius Clark was driving his gig home with his wife sitting beside him. A gig was a small open, two-wheeled carriage

St Ninian's Church.

85

pulled by one horse and used for local journeys such as by farmers going to market. Mr Clark set out in his customary good health but on the return journey complained of feeling unwell. By the time they got home, he couldn't get down from the gig without help. He got inside his house and died a few minutes afterwards.

Not everyone reached home. Mary Ann Chapman was staying with her uncle at his home in London when she died.

A more tragic departure was recorded in the *York Herald* of 22nd February 1817: 'Inhumanity and Ignorance. – On Thursday week, a poor man of the name of Wray, whose friends were removing him in a cart from Whitby to Guisborough, in the skirts of a dreary moor near a cottage, by Freebrough hill, he suddenly became so extremely unwell, they were induced to ask admittance, which was at first reluctantly granted, but the poor man growing worse, the inhuman inhabitant of the cottage compelled them to leave the place, saying that should he die there, she never durst live in the house again. They did so, but had not proceeded much farther before he expired on the public highway.'

Accidents accounted for some deaths. Tragically a little boy of five, the son of one of the alum workers near Whitby, ran gleefully towards the cliff edge and fell the whole way to the beach below it. It amazed the onlookers when rescuers lifted him up and brought him back apparently unhurt; their relief was short for the small lad died soon afterwards.

Not all Whitby's citizens had short lives; some had very long ones.

On a March Sunday in 1816 Miss Susannah Watson died at the age of ninety-two mourned by her niece, Mrs Hutchinson. In November 1812 Thomas Hall died at nearly 86; he would be widely known as he had once been landlord of the *Angel*. Mrs Skinner was 85 when she died in 1815.

In those antibioticless days, people died who would have recovered now. Almost certainly an instance of that was Dinah Medd, the daughter of a Stockton shipowner, who was staying in Whitby when she was '...cut off by a fever in the bloom of her youth.'

It was usual to paint a glowing word picture of the deceased in their obituary. So, when 68 year-old Thomas Pierson died, we learn '...in whose retired and unassuming character were united the most amiable and valuable qualities.' It sounded so much better than saying: a nice shy man.

When Sarah Sanders, daughter of Jonathan Sanders, died in 1815, her interment was in the Quaker Burial Ground as the Sanders family were faithful members of that community. The Quakers' cemetery was between Bagdale and the present Pannett Park. Captain Scoresby senior lived at 13 Bagdale quite near to the burial ground. Opposite to the terrace where he lived was Bagdale Hall, still a lovely old building with timbered ceilings; in Regency days it was subdivided into tenements. Nearby was the Roman Catholic Church, a stone building seating 300.

Considerable numbers of Whitby's population were Methodists who had a chapel, called Wesley, which was in Church Street. Older members of that community could remember the visit of Charles Wesley, the hymn-writer, when the church was opened. Although it seated 800, another building was needed and in 1814 bricklayers were at work in Scate Lane erecting a Methodist Church large enough to seat 1200. It was named Brunswick Chapel and became the regular place of worship for the Methodists although the old Wesley Church was still used occasionally.

Before the new building had been erected, Mrs Clark, wife of George Clark the bookseller, died. She was described as ' A respectable member of the Methodist Society, whose amiable domestic qualities have long endeared her to an agreeable circle of social connection.'

X X

Some Whitby Customs

A STRANGER, ARRIVING IN WHITBY on the day before Ascension Day, might be very puzzled to see a crowd of people on the shore in the upper harbour. If he pushed his way between blue-coated men and ladies in bonnets and shawls, he would be even more puzzled by what he saw. A small hedge was being constructed out of hazel twigs. The blows of a mallet mingled with the comments of the crowd: 'Another one here!' It seemed that this was an annual event and the same number of hazel twigs had to be used every year.

Then someone blew 'Out on ye!' three times on a horn. And it had to be three times.

For this was a feudal custom dating from the twelfth century. Ancient law said that the manor lands of Whitby would be forfeited if the small hedge was not made and made properly which meant that it had to continue until three tides had gone by. This was the ceremony of the Horngarth.

Whitby had many annual customs.

At Martinmas, anyone wanting a labourer, would go to Church Street where people seeking work would stand on the west side of the road. Here was a man holding a whip and another with a crook; there was a woman with a broom and another with a basting-spoon. So you knew that a groom, a shepherd a housemaid and a cook were standing there. Each of the servants seeking employment had brought a tool to advertise their skill. This was the Hiring Fair.

On December evenings carol singers, mostly women, walked from Whitby to neighbouring villages and carried with them a box, decorated with evergreen, and containing a wax doll dressed as the baby Jesus. Since most Georgian dolls had dark eyes, this would surely be more suitable for

NE view of Whitby Abbey.

the baby born in the middle eastern land than the blue-eyed baby of modern Christmas cards.

The carol singers went from house to house and were usually invited inside after singing of the divine birth.

Gingerbread played a part in most Whitby celebrations. It was made with treacle and the dough was put in moulds with pictures and sometimes people's names on them. It was certainly one of the Christmas foods.

So was frumity, a sticky dish eaten plentifully during Regency days in country areas from the Channel northwards. More than twelve tons of creed wheat were sold in Whitby Market before Christmas so that people could make frumity. The wheat was used with milk and spices for making this glutinous and popular recipe to eat on Christmas Day.

From Boxing Day to New Year's Day the young men went through the villages around Whitby performing sword dances. It is fortunate that they used wooden swords for they had no guards on them. There were six dancers with a fiddler for the music. Tradition also demanded that there should be a strangely dressed lad who was even more strangely named; he was called Bessy. Also there was a youth called the Doctor and one of the dancers was the King.

As the lads made a hexagonal shape, holding their weapons aloft, Bessy intervened and burst into the dance getting 'killed' as a punishment.

The sword dancers made their rounds and the spectators understood what was expected. 'These frolicks they continue till New Year's Day, when they spend their gains at the ale-house with the greatest innocence and mirth,' wrote someone in 1811.

It was back to work again after Twelfth Night so the day was generally known as Plough Monday. This was an excuse for some final jollifications and a plough was pulled round the town. Six men wore their white costumes to perform the sword dances all over again. Others came with them acting the roles of the miller, the doctor and the king; there was even a clown.

The chill of the January day was enlivened by a group of Madgies (which meant magpies); sometimes they were called Madgy-Pegs. These were men who dressed themselves in gowns, borrowed from mothers and wives, to knock on doors and ask for 'Plough Money'. Whitby householders obligingly handed over coins to be spent in the ale houses.

Variations of the Plough Monday customs were followed in different parts of the country but Whitby always had its own distinctive contribution to make to the old traditions.

Its young ladies seem to have been obsessed with the desire to dream about their future mates. If there was no wedding or christening to provide suitable Dreaming Bread, the romantic miss might get a couple of her friends to join her in making a Dumb Cake, presumably with much giggling. They had to mix the first egg laid by a young hen with flour and bake it over the fire. After that it was divided into three so they each had a piece. Then came the tricky bit for, having eaten part of her piece, each girl had to put the rest in the stocking she had worn on her left leg. She then walked backwards, without speaking to anyone, and put the stocking under her pillow. The dream of Mr Right was supposed to follow.

The first new moon of the year provided another opportunity to dream of her future husband. She looked at the moon through a black silk handkerchief and recited this verse.

> 'New moon! new moon! I hail thee,
> This night my true love for to see:
> Not in his best or wurst array,
> But his apparel for every day;
> That I tomorrow may him ken,
> From among all other men.'

After this she hadn't to speak to anyone else and she had to walk backwards to bed. It is not recorded if any young women really did dream of their sweethearts – nor if any of them fell downstairs!

However, we do learn many of Whitby's customs from the pen of George Young who recorded them in 1817. George Young is the historian's friend. He was a Scotsman who was appointed as minister of Cliff Lane Chapel and soon became a chronicler of Whitby. A modest man, he was also very clever. It was said of him that he had 'Far more than common knowledge of French, Italian, Greek and Hebrew, he was acquainted with Arabic, Chaldee and Syriac; and in the Anglo-Saxon language he was appealed to as an authority.' This vast linguistic skill enabled him to translate old documents and inscriptions for his *History of Whitby* which was published in 1817. He studied Bede's *Ecclesiastical History*, read documents relating to Captain Cook and explored the ruins of Grosmont Priory (now all gone).

His achievements are even more fantastic because he was born with only one hand but he said, 'I never knew the use of a left hand, and, therefore, do not feel the loss of it, having been accustomed from my earliest years to fall upon schemes for supplying the deficiency.'

St Hilda's Terrace.

91

His interests were far-reaching. He explored ancient ruins, searched for fossils, studied minerals and loved theology. It is not surprising that this cultured man with his physical courage and spiritual insight became a close friend of William Scoresby. There were a number of young men at that time living in Whitby whose intellectual pursuits and vigorous activity meant they had much in common. Another of George Young's friends was John Bird, a keen trout fisherman, a skilful artist who drew illustrations of fossils, ruins and buildings for George Young's books. He even made his own printing press and produced copies of his works on it.

These were men of inquiring mind who appreciated the beauties of nature and the finest works of man. Young described St Hilda's Terrace, then called New Buildings, as '... that beautiful street ... It consists only of one row of houses, but all of them are handsome, and some magnificent.' Eventually he went to live in one of them.

XXI

Knives and Cutters

CUSTOMS, EXCISE AND THOSE WHO wouldn't pay them made an impact on the life of Whitby.

Smugglers thrived because they were sure of a market for their goods. Among their customers were local farmers who bought their wares and turned a blind eye to activities which resulted in cheaper spirits.

The Collector of Excise was Thomas Jones, helped by his clerk, John Percy, and answerable to the supervisor, George Robinson. Evidently Mr Jones was credited with the status of a gentleman for the word 'esquire' followed his name and he purchased a gun licence. Only gentlemen were allowed the privilege of using a fowling-piece to shoot game.

On the 18th of November 1818, the York newspapers were edged with black for the death of Queen Charlotte but the king's wife was not the only person mourned in the press. The same *York Herald* also announced the death of Thomas Jones at Whitby. He evidently died in harness for he was described as Collector of Excise with no indication of having retired.

Christopher Coulson was the Collector of Customs and his office was in Sandgate. He, too, ranked as one of Whitby's gentlemen, having a licence to shoot game which cost him £3.13.6d. He had the assistance of the Revenue Cutters at sea, the Tide Surveyor in the harbour and the Riding Officers on land. Nonetheless, his job was difficult because local people did not support him, although he might sometimes get information from a paid Informer and it was difficult to get this payment money reimbursed by the Honourable Commissioners of the Customs in London.

A revenue cutter was specially designed and built for the use of the Customs so that vessels carrying smuggled goods might be chased. It had one mast carrying a mainsail attached to a boom which could be moved to enable the sail to catch the wind if it changed direction. There was also a movable bowsprit which carried another sail; a jib sail was often used as well. The cutter was armed with carronades – small cannon made at the Carron Works in Scotland.

The job of a tide-waiter was to board a ship when it docked and make sure that the goods it carried were assessed for customs duties. Tide-waiters never quite knew what a day would bring. Two of them were scouring the upper part of the harbour in December 1816 where the outgoing tide had left brown ribbon-like seaweed on the wet sand. They looked suspiciously at a coble; it was obviously an old boat. What was it doing there? Together, they moved it and the mud underneath it was disturbed. A hole had been dug there and filled in. They dug it out and found, buried in the ground, two half-ankers of gin. In all, there would be about eight gallons of the spirit.

A riding officer would rein in his horse on the cliff top and watch the shape of a boat which did not seem to be moving very far. Was it hovering? His job involved looking for hoverers; the Government was aware that such craft were often carrying brandy or other smuggled goods.

The Customs Officers were brave men. If contraband goods were seized and taken down to the Custom House, an angry crowd would follow and Sandgate became a struggling mass of people shouting and making threatening gestures whilst armed Revenue Officers protected the goods.

In 1817 barrels of smuggled gin were seized and trundled on a cart towards the office of Customs. A shouting, furious mob came behind it. The lynch pins were pulled out of the wheels and the cart fell over; the barrels burst and gin began to run down the gutters.

This was too good to lose; the crowd forgot their vindictive threats and scooped up the liquid in cupped hands or any container they could find.

Christopher Coulson was probably grateful for the burst barrels; a thirst for gin had quelled a riot.

Mr Coulson's staff included a clerk, Peter Maxwell; a comptroller, Thomas Parkin and a surveyor, Isaiah Moorsom. There were three landing-waiters, two riding-officers watching for smugglers and seven tide-waiters and boatmen.

Mr Coulson also collected taxes from the alum works and used two crews of seven men each with boats at Staithes and Robin Hood's Bay.

Old Smuggler (the Ship
Launch Inn*)*.

In 1814 the revenue he collected was at its highest but in an average year it was below nine thousand pounds.

The men responsible for Excise and Customs may have been unpopular with large sections of the community but perhaps their courage aroused admiration from some young ladies. In September 1815 Mr Fawcett, one of the Excise Officers married Miss Ripley, a Whitby bride.

Mulgrave Castle Inn in Upgang was a favourite haunt of the smugglers. In 1817 the Preventive Men went there to search for smuggled gin and found 200 tubs of it.

That same year on a Wednesday night when a March gale was blowing across the North Sea, a revenue cutter near Whitby gave chase to a smuggling vessel. A fight ensued but the ferocious storm battled against both the contenders and drove them onto the shore. It couldn't prevent bloodshed between them. The cutter had its carronades but smugglers were notoriously adept with sharp knives. The fight was later described as 'dreadful' and the end of it was a tally of eleven men killed, four from the cutter and seven of the smugglers.

Ten smugglers escaped and managed to get places on a coach. It rattled away from Whitby and passed through York without anyone in that city being aware of the 'profession' of its occupants. They reached London in safety.

The *Ship Launch Inn* in Baxtergate (now the Old Smuggler Cafe) was a sanctuary for smugglers and had an underground passage linking it to another inn. It was conveniently near the harbour and smugglers could sit under the low beamed ceilings drinking, chatting and smoking clay pipes, confident that their goods were securely hidden. Whitby contained many underground cellars and subterranean passages which were frequented by men with wooden casks on which no tax had been paid. With so many hiding places, it was easy for gin and brandy to be lodged in safety.

X X I I

A Chapter of Accidents

IT WAS LATE APRIL 1815; in Belgium British regiments were gathering to fight Napoleon, who had escaped from his exile and raised a new army. In Whitby a ferocious wind was blowing smoke and wood shavings all over the place. At sea a sloop, called the *Thomas Readman*, with a cargo of lime was struggling in heavy seas.

Her crew of three – the master, his twelve year-old son and his daughter's fiancé, had come from Sunderland. They pitched about in an ocean of deep black troughs and curling white horses. They were making for Whitby to find refuge in its harbour when a precipitous wave struck the mast, tearing it from the deck. The vessel capsized.

At about seven o'clock the hull was washed up on the shore and when Whitby men inspected it they found the boy's body among the lime. There was no sign of the two men and their bodies were never discovered; they had drowned when the ship turned turtle.

A fishing boat called *The Brothers* came to grief off Whitby and the same storm claimed a Whitby ship, the *Heart of Oak*, which belonged to Mr Smales. Gideon Smales was a member of the family firm which built ships, owned ships and supplied masts and spars for ships. She was commanded by Captain Ridley but all aboard her lost their lives when the *Heart of Oak* went down near Staithes.

Whitby ships could be lost much farther off than that. In August 1817 the *William Bathgate*, of Whitby, was wrecked one Sunday morning on Brighton's pebbly beach. Like Staithes, Brighton was once a fishing village but it had become much more. The Prince Regent had built a fantastic Chinese-style palace for himself there and it had become a fashionable resort. It also became the graveyard of one of Whitby's ships that August morning.

XXIII

At Home in Whitby

FORTUNATELY MOST SHIPS DID GET safely back to port. There was the welcome silhouette of the abbey on the clifftop, a little more of it than we can see for it still had the centre tower and an arch over the west doorway. Eyes scanned the hillside behind it and discovered Larpool Hall. That is still there but trees and buildings hide it, although it retains its doorway (now rather hidden by a Victorian porch) and inside the hall the original cantilever staircase still leads to a lovely Venetian window.

All the higgledy-piggledy roofs of Whitby greeted the returning mariners. There was a shortage of space on land near the harbour so, when the population increased, they couldn't build tidy terraces. People,

Whitby Abbey c1785.

98

whose houses had gardens, found they could make extra money by building a small house on their land and letting it to another family. Some of the charming alleys were created to give access to these hidden homes.

Some houses were divided horizontally to make what we should call flats. Each had its own timber balcony with an outside staircases – much prettier than a modern lift and much wetter in bad weather.

Many quaint corners have disappeared. In Haggersgate, Bakehouse Yard and Pier Lane are all that remain from the medley of yards leading to Cliff Street.

In Cliff Street, as we can still see, the houses faced each other across the road but, because the hill is so steep, those on the east side were lower than those on the west. Railings protected the path in front of them and their ground floors were level with these fences. From the back upstairs windows there would be a dramatic view of the abbey. The houses on the west side of Cliff Street were taller at the back than the front and numbers 40-43 still have doorways with identical fanlights.

Pedestrians had to be careful not to fall into someone's area. This was a small yard in front of the basement kitchen. Poplar Row, behind Skinner Street, still has two pairs of houses with areas and steps bridging them to reach the front doors. Skinner Street was a road of elegant houses but only a very few are left now. Silver Street has fared better. Well Close Square had some smart houses; one of them, Tanshelf, still has its Doric columns; it was twenty-two years old when the Regency began.

There were some fashionable homes in Bagdale and one of them was for sale in April 1813. It had two basement kitchens, three reception rooms on the ground floor and five bedrooms plus suitable rooms for servants'. There was a front and a back garden with an outhouse for brewing homemade beer and a stable for two horses.

Most of Church Street was much narrower than now. As carts rumbled past, people would see the wheels directly beside their front windows. When two carts passed each other, the drivers needed to take care that their wheels didn't lock together. One hopes it did not lead to any road rage.

The crews of homecoming ships would look gratefully at the whole panorama of undulating tiles, narrow bricks, wooden steps and cobblestones. These were the homes of friends and family, of alum workers and shipwrights, whalers and shopkeepers, fishermen and ostlers, milliners and innkeepers, servants and stonemasons, parsons and printers, cooks and bankers.

Henrietta Street.

Flowergate.

Cottages with archway.

Honeysuckle fanlight.

101

As the ship sailed along the greyish-brown water of the Esk, the narrow ghauts and gabled roofs were reflected in the river. This was home and all the hardships of the voyage were over. We can imagine the returning sailor striding up Henrietta Street past houses and cottages, sash windows, bow windows and small Yorkshire Lights to the one little house which held all that was dear to him.

Galleried dwellings.

XXIV

Pew and Pulpit

ON A SUMMER SUNDAY MORNING when worshippers climbed the steps towards St Mary's Church, the sapphire sea stretched out to a hazy horizon and white blobs of seagulls were discernible riding on the gently moving water. Some people arrived panting at the top of the 'stairs', men respectfully removed their hats, all trooped into the old church. It was the sort of day when the buzzing of an insect, trapped inside a building, induced soporific tendencies in the people who heard it.

Lengthy sermons could drone on for well over an hour in those days; the vocabulary in the *Prayer Book* and the Authorized Version may have seemed strange to untutored minds but men who spent their working hours in boats could identify with the fishermen who became the first disciples. It is not inappropriate that doodling fingers carved boats under the pew ledges.

It must have been fun to watch the surreptitious carving of a sloop or brig taking shape whilst the sonorous pulpit voice continued a lengthy dissertation. People sitting still in family pews in the centre block of the south transept might steal an occasional glance towards the less comfortable pews near the wall and be aware of a slight scratching sound. Children, whose feet didn't even touch the floor, probably longed for a knife or even a nail so they could at least scratch their initials but adult eyes would have observed too much.

We can still see some of these graffiti; many are older than the Regency and may have provided inspiration for the carvers of that time, one of whom put his initials I.S. in 1816 on a pew in the back of the south transept. Not all the carvings were of ships; one of the Ugglebarnby pews has a crude picture of a church accompanied by numerous initials. Some village lads certainly made their mark.

Pulpit.

Chandelier.

Regency windows at St Marys.

As you entered the church you might think you had embarked on a ship and you wouldn't be far wrong. Years earlier Whitby's population had grown too big for the twelfth century church. Her shipwrights had constructed galleries to accommodate all the extra people. Even the ceiling looked like the top of a deck. Sailors would feel at home in these surroundings so like a cabin without a heaving floor. The same skills which built a brig had sawn and planed and painted a place of worship.

In 1819 additional pews were added to the north side. Permission for this extension had to be granted by the diocese and the cross-shape of the church was lost by the addition. The expense was met from an auction. Folk who wanted to purchase a pew there for their family's use went to bid. Many people thought it would be pleasant to have one of the new pews and so excitement rose with the bids and £991 was raised. A grant of £300 was paid to the churchwardens which enabled a furthur 47 pews to be made for the use of anyone who could not afford to buy a seat. Certain pews were assigned to people from nearby villages which did not have their own churches.

The church had no organ but most country churches had a band playing in a gallery so there was nothing strange about Whitby having no organ.

In winter it would be cosy to worship there. Attached to the end of the pew was a simple iron candlestick making it easier to read a prayer book. However the chandelier in the centre lit up the interior and gave one a view of the vicar, the Rev James Andrew, at the top of the three-tier pulpit. It also enabled one to see other members of the congregation. The ship's apprentices (teenage boys learning about navigation and living in a captain's home) sat in the west gallery. The person conducting the service was below the vicar in the middle tier of the pulpit and the parish clerk sat in the bottom layer. If you wanted to see the vicar, you had to look upwards although the lord of the manor's family did not need to do that. The Cholmley family pew stood on pillars with its back to the chancel, an irreverent position but one which enabled them to concentrate on the sermon.

It became necessary to produce a speaking trumpet for the benefit of the vicar's wife, a deaf lady who would otherwise miss her husband's homily.

The church was crowded and a very busy place. In 1816 there were 348 baptisms, 253 burials and 119 marriages. George Young thought it was a pity they were unable to restore the larger, ruined church

Whitby Abbey drawn by H. Gastineau.

107

belonging previously to the Abbey. Many people would not have agreed with him. Regency folk loved medieval ruins and some even considered that Henry VIII had done England a good turn by dissolving the monasteries and leaving a plethora of crumbling arches and ivied walls. More significantly, the inhabitants of Whitby wanted to worship where their parents and grandparents and ancestors before them had knelt to pray. It was comforting to walk past their gravestones and be aware of the continuity of all life. Some, like the Moorsom family, had monuments inside the building. All responded each Sunday to the pealing of the six bells which called them from mundane tasks to commune with the Creator.

In this peaceful church some of the weathered seamen felt that awareness of the spiritual which they had felt on a calm and moonlit sea.

Bibliography

Abranson, Erik: *Sailors of the Great Sailing ships.*
Baines, Edward: *History of Yorkshire.* 1822.
Barker, Rosalin: *The Book of Whitby.*
Barron, Capt. William: *Old Whaling Days.* 1895.
Betjeman, John: *English Parish Churches.*
Brown, Harold: *A Walk Round Whitby.*
Cunnington, Willett and Phillis: *The History of Underclothes.*
Daysh, G.H.J.: *A Survey of Whitby and the Surrounding Area.*
Dykes, Jack: *Yorkshire's Whaling Days.*
English, Thomas H.: *Introduction to the Collection and History of Whitby Prints.* 1931.
Gaskell, Mrs: *Sylvia's Lovers.*
Gaskin, Robert Tate: *The Old Seaport of Whitby.*
Geikie, Sir Archibald: *Annals of the Royal Society Club.* 1917.
Humble, A.F.: *The Rowing Life-Boats of Whitby.*
Humble, A.F.: *Prints of Old Whitby.*
Hutchinson, William: *A Treatise on Practical Seamanship.* 1777.
Jackson, Gordon: *The British Whaling Trade.*
Jeffrey, Shaw: *Whitby Lore and Legend.*
Kendall, Hugh P.: *The Streets of Whitby and their Associations.*
Lubbock, Basil: *Arctic Whalers.*
Lyth, John: *Glimpses of Early Methodism in York.* 1885.
Major, Alan: *Maritime Antiques.*
Morrison, Alan: *Alum.*
O'Brian, Patrick: *Joseph Banks. A Life.*
Payne, Fred: *Whaling and Whitby.*
Pearson, Paul D.: *The Esk.*
Pile, Albert T.: *Buildings of Old Whitby.*
Pope, Dudley: *England Expects.*
Pope, Dudley: *Life in Nelson's Navy.*
Preston C.: *Captain William Scoresby.*

109

Scoresby, William: *Journal of a Voyage to the Northern Whale Fishery*. 1823.
Smith Graham: *King's Cutters. The Revenue Service and the War Against Smuggling*.
Stamp, Tom and Cordelia: *Whitby and District*.
Stamp, Tom and Cordelia: *William Scoresby. Arctic Scientist*.
Sythes, D.G.: *Around Whitby*. (Archive Photographers Series.)
Tindale, John: *Owlers, Hoverers and Revenue Men*.
Ventress, Monica: *Admiral Sir Robert Moorsom. 1760-1835*.
Vickers, Noreen: *Whitby*.
Vince, John: *Power Before Steam*.
Waters, Colin: *A History of Whitby's Pubs, Inns and Taverns*.
Waters, Colin: *Bygone Whitby*.
Waters, Colin: *Whitby. A Pictorial History*.
Watson, J. Steven: *The Reign of George III*.
Weatherill, Richard: *The Ancient Port of Whitby and Its Shipping*. 1908.
White, Andrew: *A History of Whitby*.
White, Andrew: *The Buildings of Georgian Whitby*.
White, Andrew: *Carvings of Ships in Whitby Parish Church*.
Whitworth, Alan: *Yorkshire Windmills*.
Young, George: *A Picture of Whitby*. 1840.
Young, George: *History of Whitby*. 1816.

Documents and Other Original Sources.

Cary's Roads. 1819. Gazeteer.
Day Book – Robert Campion and John Campion. 1791-1806.
Index of Ratepayers of Ruswarp. 1811-1820.
Index of those Receiving Relief. 1813-1819.
Masting Book of the Smales Firm. Whitby. 1750-1871.
The New Seaman's Guide and Coaster's companion. 1815.
Overseer of the Poor Account Book.
The Whitby Times. 1888.
The York Chronicle. 1811.
The York Herald. 1811-1819.

Index